T0113783

Riddles, Folktales and Proverbs from Cameroon

Comfort Ashu

Langaa Research & Publishing CIG
Mankon, Bamenda

Publisher:
Langaa RPCIG
Langaa *Research & Publishing Common Initiative Group*
P.O. Box 902 Mankon
Bamenda
North West Region
Cameroon
Langaagrp@gmail.com
www.langaa-rpcig.net

Distributed outside N. America by African Books Collective
orders@africanbookscollective.com
www.africanbookcollective.com

Distributed in N. America by Michigan State University Press
msupress@msu.edu
www.msupress.msu.edu

ISBN: 9956-578-49-5

© Comfort Ashu 2010

DISCLAIMER
All views expressed in this publication are those of the author and do not necessarily reflect the views of Langaa RPCIG.

CONTENT

INTRODUCTION

Welcome Wonderer, Welcome Home

In the land of strangers
Wither thou art gone
Hear afar voice calling
My son! My son!

Come home! Come home!
See the arms still open
Open to embrace thee
Eyes of love are on thee

My son! My son!
Come home! Come home!
Come to my bosom
Come and feel the warmth

Of your true mother
Wipe my fallen tears
My son! My son!
Welcome home! Welcome home!

P ermit me my dear readers to use the above stanzas to express my joy in receiving my lost piece of art. It was pirated to Nigeria where it went out of sight, it got lost Thank God, it has been recovered; welcome home.

In 1984, Mr. Etim U. Akaduh, a writer and publisher with Mason Publishing Company came to Cameroon for business. In the course of the meetings that he had with writers, he accepted to-edit my work jointly with Dr. A. K. Mosongo of the Buea Linguistic Centre. It is on this basis that he took my manuscripts and the illustrations to Nigeria.

Sad enough, when he arrived Nigeria, he edited the material and published it as "Ayito", a collection of folktales that he placed in the market-since 1984 without the author's knowledge.

Cameroonians studying in Nigeria stumbled on it in libraries and bookshops and they got copies for me. Efforts to track down the pirate have failed and like any mother, the discovery of a lost child brings joy even if it comes with hardship.

It is for this reason that I have revisited the text with modifications. The book is presented in three parts. Part I (A) has folktales on animals and Part II (B) has folktales that highlight the image of a woman in the African society. This covers Riddles, and Part III is on our thoughts through proverbs.

The rich content leads to the title - African Literature for Schools, a totality of African Oral Literature.

****

In the olden days, after a day's work in the farms, children and parents returned home feeling worn out. As a sort of evening entertainment, children of the same family, compound or village then gathered round a story-teller to listen to folk tales and riddles. This was common in every African home.

The listeners participate with joy by joining in the songs and choruses. Sometimes the children were given the opportunity to tell stories that they had known while the adult story-teller listened attentively in order to add more details where necessary.

In telling these stories and riddles, children were expected to learn something through all those activities connected with the customs, environment, language and religious practices of their people. Unless children benefit from these story-telling sessions, the story-teller does not consider himself successful. Most folk-tales are about the Tortoise and children of all ages are always delighted to listen. The tales on human beings highlight the image of these sexes as perceived in the two sets of folktales.

This book provides children with stories, riddles and some proverbs that parents ought to have told their children at -home but have failed because of their present day busy schedules. Teachers will fill that vacuum at school as they guide the children in reading the stories, riddles and proverbs in their second language - English. As an instructional tool, this collection will foster literacy, promote cultural awareness and create situations where learners share with one another their personal experiences and traditions.

PART ONE

AYITO

Once upon a time, there lived a great chief whose name was Ayito. He ruled over a large chiefdom and lived in a large palace. He owned a large estate and most of the wealth of the land belonged to him. As an Ekpe chief, he was entitled to marry many women.

Every morning, the best palm wine from his estate was brought to him and once a month, his attendants brought all the beautiful girls of the land to his palace as prospective wives of the chief. As it was the tradition, all these beautiful girls had to be initiated into Nkim and Ndem before chief Ayito made his final selection of his wives.

In order to train the girls to dance to all the tunes of the tribal dances, Ayito kept a permanent orchestra in his palace. The band played music every day. He also threw parties for his would - be wives and the chief-makers three days a week.

One fine day, Ayito ordered his town crier to summon all his subjects to the palace. The town crier beat his drum. Within a short period, everybody was in the palace.

When all the people sat down, according to their ranks, Ayito raised his Ekpe stick:

My name is Ayito, Chief of Ekpe
And Chief of this land!
Heyjey! Heyjey! Heyjey!
Esong miaco! Hey jeh!
Bakwindi! Heyjey!
Mboco! Heyjey! Bari O!

The assembly responded, *"Wah!!!"*

After this initial address, the gathering was silent.

Ayito then rose from his throne and addressed the people. He told them 'that he had decided to amend the law of the land slightly.

"From this day", he began "no female shall eat meat. Women shall eat fish and men shall eat meat. That is what I have for you"

The law was strange. Nobody could question Ayito's wisdom. Everybody thought he must have good reasons for passing such a law. He was the wise man of the land and so everything he said had to be accepted without question. So the people accepted the new law of the land.

For many years, women cooked meat for their husbands and male children. The women ate their fish with relish. Since there was enough game for men to hunt and enough fish for women to catch, nobody complained.

But after two years, misfortune struck Ayito's land. An epidemic killed all the animals in the land. From other lands, people feared allowing their cattle, goats and sheep to enter Ayito's territory.

Men spent several nights hunting but could not find any animals to kill. Not even a squirrel or a rat could be found in the forest. The men got upset. How long could they live on vegetables as fish was not to be eaten by men? What a bad law!

The women had no problem, the rivers and the sea still flowed and so there was fish in abundance. The women sympathized with their men but how could they cook good meals for them without meat? Women ate well and looked healthy but the men grew skinnier and anaemic. If only the law could be revoked so that the men could eat fish and live healthier and happier.

The awful condition of the men could not continue

indefinitely. So some inquisitive men began to ask what the basis of Ayito's law was. The simple-minded men thought their ancestors were angry and suggested that some libation should' be offered to them. Libation was offered but the situation bore no fruits.

Ayito's law was beginning to infringe on his administration. Everybody questioned publicly why men should starve when there was enough fish in the land to feed both men and women. Ayito himself thought in the same manner, but did not-have the courage to amend the law. It was painful and strange for a ruler to starve himself in that way.

Then one evening, Ayito went to his first wife's kitchen and stealthily opened her pot of soup. The flavour reached his nostrils making his mouth watery. He then decided to take a piece of fish, So he opened the biggest pot. Just then his wife appeared and questioned him. Ayito pleaded with the woman and begged her not to raise any alarm. He then confessed to his wife that he was suffering seriously because of not eating meat. And so the woman allowed her husband to eat the fish a second time, promising not to reveal his offense.

But before day break, a little bird which had hidden somewhere flew to the roof of the Town Hall and began to sing a song;

Ekpe juju
Ayito! Ayito!
Ekpe chief has broken Ekpe law
Ayito! Ayito!
Chief of the land has broken the law of the land.
Ayito! Ayito!
That women eat fish
That men eat meat
Ayito! Ayito!

Ayito has eaten meat and has eaten fish
Ayito! Ayito!
Ekpe chief has broken Ekpe law

The entire chiefdom was alerted with interest. Within a short time, people gathered in the Town Hall. In shame, the elders of the land began to ponder over the crime committed by their ruler.

"A fine! A heavy fine!" shouted the young men. Everybody agreed that their chief should pay a fine, but their problem was what type of fine. So the elders went into committees. Soon they came out with the conclusion that their chief should pay a fine of one cow, one goat and ten jugs of wine.

Immediately, everybody moved to the chiefs palace and the decision of the elders was announced to the chief and all present. Ayito tried to plead with the people, explaining what had happened. But nobody could listen to him. At last, Ayito paid the fine and learnt that nobody was above the law.

Ekpe: An Ekpe chief may not necessarily be the village chief. The title - 'Ekpe' chief refers to anyone who purchases an Ekpe lodge; Ekpe sometimes called "Nyankpe" or "Ngeb" is a social, political and sacred society among the Bafondos, Banyangi. Ejagham tribes of Manyu in Cameroon and the Cross River State of Nigeria.

Nkirn and Ndem are women's associations among the Bayang and Ejagham tribes of Manyu in Cameroon and the Ejagham of Nigeria. The initiated members are given herbs and training that makes them good dancers of a special status, hence the bride wealth of iiueh u omen as higher and heavier fines were levied for adults:

Moral: "The law is no respecter of persons. Those who make the law must abide by the law."

Questions for Discussion

1. What quality made Ayito a great man in his land?
2. Do you find the same qualities in your riders? If your answer is no, what are the differences between the qualities of Ayito and those of the rulers in your locality?
3. What crime did Ayito commit?
4. Who told his people?
5. How was he punished?
6. Discuss the sayings: "The law is no respecter of persons", and "those who make (he law must abide by the law ".
7. Do you know any leader among your people who committed a similar crime like Ayito's?
8. How was he punished?
9. Explain the words—anaemic, revoked.

THE OWL AND THE PEACOCK
(A Love Contest)

Mother Owl and Mother Peacock were very good friends. Each of them had an only daughter whom they loved dearly. The two mothers met often to discuss their common problems of having only a daughter. Whenever they met, the women always expressed the love they had for their only daughters.

One day, Mother Peacock suggested to her friend that they should hatch a plan in order to find out if the two girls really loved their mothers too. So they decided to pretend to be dead.

"That is a good idea", "commented mother Owl. "My daughter will scream and mourn. She will starve herself for days, if not weeks". She added, with satisfaction.

"I have another suggestion" said Mother Peacock. "Before we lie in bed as if we were dead, let us send our daughters to fetch some water from the stream".

Mother owl again supported her friend's suggestion. So the women got to their homes and ordered the girls to go and fetch drinking water.

As soon as the girls were away, their mothers went into their beds and laid there stiff, pretending to be dead.

Daughter Peacock was a smart girl. At once, she ran to fetch her water and returned home with her calabash full to the brim.

On her arrival, she found her mother lying in bed. The girl put down her calabash and touched her mother. But the woman was fast asleep. "Mama! Mama! Mama!" the girl called and then shouted, but there was no answer, only silence. "Mama must be fast asleep[1]" she murmured. Then she felt afraid and so called again, this time louder. Still, there was no reply. Mother Peacock did not wake up. So the girl shook her mother's hand and to her surprise, it was stiff and cold. "She touched her mother's forehead. Mama did not show any sign of life. Mother Peacock was not even breathing, she took it that her mother was dead!

At once, the girl jumped up as if in a fainting fit, and fell on the floor, rolled herself over and then burst out screaming.

In that heart-burning mood, the girl flew out to announce the misfortune to the rest of the birds in the neighbourhood. Within a short time, all the birds of the air sang loudly the good deeds of Mother Peacock. The girl stood by her mother's supposed corpse shedding more tears. Not long, while the girl was planning how her mother should be buried, the woman got up. It was a wonderful reunion.

Not long, the Owl's daughter returned from the spring and found her mother looking dead. Immediately, the girl burst into a fit of joy as she sang:

So you are dead?
What a relief!
No more errands,
No more carrying of water
No more scolding from a mother,
Who is always ill.
Well, as from today
All her property will be mine
There she lies as cold as ice!

On hearing -the evil words and wishes from her daughter, Mother Owl immediately got out of her bed.

"You are a wicked child!" cried Mother Owl, as she took hold of her daughter and slapped her.

And so, Mother peacock won the contest.

Questions for Discussion
1. How did Mother Peacock and Mother Owl test their daughters' love for them?
2. How did Daughter peacock react to her mother's mock-dead?
3. What reasons did Daughter Owl give for not loving her mother?

KING TORTOISE AND THE ANT

Long, long ago, all the creatures of the earth lived in one kingdom where Tortoise was the king. They engaged in hunting, farming and fishing together. Whatever they got from their toils was enjoyed by everybody. They also built their houses and constructed their markets and roads communally.

One day, the kingdom decided to construct a road to their communal farms to facilitate the transportation of food to their homes. This job was embarked upon just before the rains were over. King Tortoise inspected the work and was satisfied. As a sort of compensation and in order to make his subjects get ready for the very demanding job of harvesting, he asked them to observe a period of rest. This was gladly accepted.

After the rest," it was time for the harvest. They harvested yams, plantains, cassava and cocoyams. They harvested pepper and fruits of all types. And according to tradition, everybody brought the best of his or her crops to the King's palace in readiness for the annual feast. The King's storage rooms were packed full with plantains, cocoyams, yams, beans, and all sorts of vegetables and fruits. A date was then fixed for the feast.

On the day of the feast, the King provided plenty of wine. Before the ordinary citizens came, the Chief Councillors of the king discovered that there was no fish to prepare the food; and that which was already prepared, the women used meat. So they reported the situation to the king. King Tortoise quickly ordered his town crier to sound his gong. On hearing this gong, the citizens assembled at the palace. The king announced the shortage of fish and asked that everybody must go and fish. The order was obeyed at once. They took out their nets, baskets and fish lines. In groups of ten, twenty, thirty, they invaded the streams, ponds and rivers.

Some types of food had already been prepared before the councillors discovered a shortage of fish. Somebody had to watch over the food. So Black Ant was appointed the day watchman for the food store. This appointment was unanimously approved by all because the ant by nature is a busy creature and hardly sleeps. Moreover, the ant eats very little food.

"When everybody had gone fishing, Black Ant sat at the entrance of the door, very alert. The fishing expedition took longer than was anticipated and the Ant remained faithful to his job. But later in the day, the Ant got tired and fell into a deep sleep. This was natural. But while the poor ant was sleeping, King Tortoise sneaked into the food store to eat the best slices of meat.

King Tortoise dished out the best of each food prepared. He took the livers, kidneys, breasts and all the other delicious and most respected parts of all animals and fowls. He sat down at one corner of the store and ate to his satisfaction. Then he turned to the wine and selected the best. He drank just enough to avoid being discovered. He was really satisfied. Then, he sneaked out of the store.

In the evening, everybody came home with the fish. The women prepared the fish and carried everything again to the store. To everybody's surprise, the food store was still locked. They knocked and knocked, but there was no answer from within. The Ant was fast asleep. They knocked harder. The Ant then got up sluggishly and slowly opened the door.

The King and his counsellors entered first to inspect the food and decide how the sharing was to be done. To their surprise, part of the food had been eaten. It was baffling to the ant. First, he could not understand what had happened.

"Who has done this?" the counsellors asked furiously

"I don't know", replied the ant.

"You don't know? King Tortoise asked very sternly.

"You must know" everybody said in a chorus, "You were left here to keep watch over the food while we strained ourselves to catch fish", one of the elders added.

The palace became rowdy. Everybody spoke at the top of his voice. Everybody was itching to express his views and to prescribe punishment for the ant. Some suggested that the ant be sent on exile. Others said 'he should be tried first, before punishment was emitted. The excessive noise came under control only when the town crier sounded his usual gong to call for silence. Silence reigned.

Everybody turned to look at the king who announced his verdict in a shrill voice. Before he passed the verdict, he drew the attention of the whole assembly to the fact that the Ant was appointed a day watchman for the food store and consequently was exempted from going for fishing. Therefore his punishment for not doing his job well had to be severe so as to set an example for the whole kingdom.

To be fair to the Ant, the king asked the assembly to suggest a befitting punishment for him. Some said the Ant should be flogged. Others suggested that he should pay a fine. Those who were very annoyed with the crime said they did not want to see the ant in their kingdom anymore. Then in his witty manner. King Tortoise disagreed with all his subjects and argued that what they had suggested would not have a lasting effect on the Ant. As a permanent punishment, King Tortoise called it quits when he announced that he would curse the ant with foul odour. Immediately, the king ordered the Ant to lie under his feet. He then polluted the air and this offensive smell stuck onto the Ant. That is why till this day, the black Ant has that offensive smell.

Question for Discussion
1. Who stole the food?
2. Why did the animals not eat their food according to schedule?
3. Was the black ant rightly punished? Why?
4. Imagine you were in an animal kingdom; how would you describe the behaviour of those animals?
5. Explain - communally, transportation, itching, as used in the text.

THE HARE AND THE LION

One fine morning, the Hare set out from his home for a walk. The sun was bright and so the flowers bloomed, making neighbouring grass look sweet. In such good weather conditions, the Hare thought he could spring up high and jump on everything on his way to express his joy. And so he skipped over rocks, grass and shrubs as he went.

Before he realized where he was, he had jumped on the Lion who was basking himself in the sun. Immediately, the Lion stretched out his paw, grabbed the tiny Hare and glanced sternly at his face.

"You tiny fellow! How dare you disturb my rest. I, King of the beasts? What can you say in defence" of your insolent self?" he shook the little Hare forward and backwards and hare gnashed his teeth in despair.

"Can't you say something?" Lion asked, still looking stern. Hare shivered and gasped for words.

"Don't you know what to say?" Lion inquired as he still shook Hare from side to side.

In fright, Hare replied with a quivering voice, "Sir, I did not mean to disturb you, please forgive me".

"No! I can't forgive you, 1 must eat you now! The other day, at the conference in Elephant's house, you laughed at me. What was the fun in what I said?"" he enquired.

Sir, it will be unfair if you eat me'\ replied the Hare. "I jumped on you in error and I have asked for forgiveness. Secondly, your remark on the laughter in the conference at Elephant's house surprises me because I can't remember that I did laugh at you. Instead, I fell out with friends who laughed at you. "So you know those who laughed at me. Should it be Tortoise?" he asked.

After a long pause, Hare suggested to the Lion to invite all the animals to his residence. "At that meeting, I assure you that I will show you those animals who made ridiculous remarks about you. Some called you wicked Jew. Others styled you a tyrant" Hare added and the Lion nodded in satisfaction. So he set hare free.

Early the next morning, Lion came out of his den and made a bull-like roar. The irregular roar came floating down the hill top, while the thrilling clamour grew louder and nearer as all the animals woke up from sleep to listen to the Lion's invitation.

"What must be wrong with Lion?" every animal murmured, while preparing to start the journey to the Lion's den. Very soon, the animals began arriving at the Lion's den. Birds from all parts of the forest came. They were led by the Hornbill, Ostrich, Hawk and the Parrot. Not long after the birds had arrived, the animals of the forest began to come in. They were led by the Elephant, Buffalo, Leopard, Antelope, Monkey, Squirrel, Pig, Goat and others. Some of the animals ran, others hopped and even the wriggling Python was there with all his relatives of the reptile family. Finally, Crocodile arrived with all the water animals. Then came the right time for Lion to address his audience because the audience was quite encouraging. Yet. he was restrained by Hare who suggested a roll call to ensure that everyone 'was present. Without hesitation, Lion accepted the suggestion. He asked Hare to conduct the roll call. He started with the birds and reptiles and soon discovered that they were all present. It was tedious doing the same for the animals that lived in water and those in the forest. All the same, he finished, started with the small creatures like Snail and the Squirrel, to the big animals like the Whale and Elephant. In going through the exercise, he discovered that Tortoise and Fox were absent,

By this time, Tortoise was on his way to the den but because his limbs were short, he could not arrive in time. However, Dog was instructed to go first for Fox because he lived farther away and to call on Tortoise on his way back. Dog listened to the instructions attentively before leaving. All those present were assured that Dog would arrive at his destination in time. But not long after leaving the den, he found a heap of cooked palm nuts by a stream.

Just at a glance, his appetite got kindled, and without bothering that the rest of the animals were waiting for him, he ate a nut and because it tasted nice, he got a second. And so he continued eating the nuts until it was dark. Meanwhile Tortoise had arrived at the Lion's den, and many who saw him thought he came on Dog's invitation.

At length. Dog left the palm nuts and continued on his mission dashing into the under bush and speeding through the forest to arrive in lime. At one time, he came across a trail junction and had a problem whose trail it was. For some time, he had his nose to the ground sniffing through the trails. At last, he discovered the right trail. He ran some distance, passing through the roughest ground, difficult gullies with the most tangled bits of under-bush. At last, he found Fox.

He delivered the message and after a few minutes of rest, they left for the Lion's den. It was dark and all the animals had been waiting for long. However, they were happy to see Dog come in with Fox.

"It's you! It's you we've been waiting for", the animals cried. For a second, the eager animals were waiting to hear why they were invited. When all was quiet, Hare asked the Lion to instruct all the animals to sit according to their sizes to enable him see them well.

This idea was wisely designed to hide away from the Lion. Without giving the suggestion a second thought, Lion made his announcement, asking all the animals to sit according to their various sizes.

The big animals such as the Elephant, Rhino, Hippopotamus, Whale, sat together and the small ones like the squirrel, Hare, Tortoise, were kept quite a distance from the big ones.

When all the animals got settled according to their sizes, Giraffe with his long neck was appointed to see if every group was represented and everyone present. He stretched out his neck and turned it from side to side. "Everybody is present" he announced.

"Tine, little Hare, where is he?" asked Lion.

"I'm here sir, sitting beside the other small animals" Hare replied.

"Will you now show me the person who made those ridiculous remarks about me when we were at the conference?" Lion asked.

With a shivering voice, Hare replied, "It was Hog who laughed at you"

"The what! H-o-g? What does he take me for?" The Lion leaped angrily towards Hog, and both of them vanished in the grass while the cunning hare ran into the opposite direction as fast as he could.

And so the hare was able to escape from the wicked Lion.

Questions for Discussion
1. Where did the hare go on the fine morning and what happened?
2. Why did the Lion refuse to forgive the Hare?
3. How did the animals react to the Lion's irregular roar?

~ -

4. Which animals were absent at the first meeting and how did they come to know about the meeting?

5. Discuss the Dog's errand to the Fox

6. What tricks did the Hare play to set himself free?

7. Get the class to write out and later act a scene of two characters - Lion (big pupil) and a Hare (small pupil)

THE TIE - TIE BRIDGE

One evening, Leopard went out to hunt. He went to a nearby river with the hope that he would catch one of those animals which frequented there to drink. Unfortunately for him, no animal went there to drink that evening. Not even crabs came out of their holes. Since he was hungry, Leopard Bad to look for something else to eat. He searched the right hand side of the bank, yet nothing moved. Then, as if by chance, he looked to the left side of the river bank and there he saw some leaves shaking.

'There must be an animal near those leaves", he murmured. Slowly and slowly, Leopard moved until he came to the-spot where the leaves were shaking. 'Behold! Spider was there building his web. He was a big spider, big enough to make good supper for Leopard. Leopard quickly grabbed spider and was about to put him into his mouth when the Spider said, "Please leopard, may I tell you something?"

"Say it quickly. I'm hungry", replied the Leopard.

"I am full of faeces", said Spider. "And it will not be nice for you to eat me in this state. Allow me empty my bowels first". Spider's words made Leopard's mouth sour. He would not eat rotten matter. So he released Spider and asked him to empty all the rot that was in his stomach.

Once released, Spider started to expel his web while Leopard watched patiently for him to finish. As the web was being excreted. Spider went up the trees, across the branches and so doing, formed a neatly woven web across the river.

Leopard who was hungry, angry and impatient asked "Does it take you so long to empty your bowels?

23

"Yes", said Spider. "You know we spiders eat very much". As he said that, he continued his journey to the other side of the river. The river was wide and deep and Leopard could not cross it.

While on the other side of the river. Spider said to Leopard, "I have now finished my work. You can now make a meal of me. The Leopard stood there dumbfounded. He was surprised that a little creature like the Spider could make a fool of him. Nevertheless, he remained there contemplating what next to do in order to have supper that evening.

Spider was about to take a rest under a leaf when he saw a hunter walking slowly towards him. He drew the attention of the hunter to the Leopard across the bridge. The hunter saw the Leopard, looked for a good position under the trees, took a good aim and fired.

"Kwa-Kum", the gun went. "Kwa-Kum", it went a second time. The two shots* got the bullet right into the Leopard and he fell dead. Spider and the hunter both rejoiced to see Leopard dead.

But killing the Leopard across the river was one thing, and taking it home to get village decoration was another. That was the problem. But the hunter must know how Spider crossed the river.

"You said the Leopard wanted to eat you on the other bank of the river?"

"Yes", replied the spider.

"How then did you escape to this bank?"

"Look up there", Spider pointed to his web.

"How did you do that?" the hunter enquired surprisingly.

"Well, just watch me go over it again" said the Spider.

The Spider climbed up one of the trees, and came to his web. With more of his excretion, he reinforced his web until he came to the opposite bank. He climbed down another tree there and came to where the Leopard lay dead. Like in a joke, he touched the Leopard but the animal was really dead. The Spider then came back to meet the hunter who confirmed that he had learnt a new skill from the Spider.

The hunter and the Spider then parted company. The hunter went back to his village and announced that he had killed a Leopard and wanted some people to help him construct a tie-tie bridge across the river in order to bring the Leopard home.

Some volunteers followed him with ropes and ladders. At the river bank, he taught them what he had learnt from the Spider. They built a tie-tie bridge, crossed over it and carried the Leopard home. A great feast followed to rejoice over the new skill they had acquired—the building of a tie-tie bridge and the killing of a Leopard.

Questions for Discussion

1. What was Leopard going to do by the river-side?
2. Who did Leopard See by the river-side? What was he doing?
3. Why did Spider decide to deceive the Leopard?
4. What did the spider really do to escape the grip of Leopard?
5. Explain the expression: "The hunter became the hunted" How is it true in this story?
6. Why did the hunter rejoice when he shot the Leopard dead?
7. What skill did man learn from the Spider?
8. What is used by women, fishermen and others which resemble a tie-tie bridge?

THE GRINDING STONE

Long, long, ago, in a very big forest, there lived a Tortoise and a Pig. The two animals were very good friends. They carried on their hunting together. Whenever they killed any animals they shared the animals equally. Their homes were near each other.

One day, the Tortoise lost his grandmother, so he went to borrow ten bags of money from .his friend the Pig. He wanted to use the money for the burial ceremony of his grandmother. The Tortoise promised to refund all the money after two months. The Tortoise buried his grandmother and finished all the funeral rites.

Unfortunately, for the Tortoise, one month after the burial, his mother - in - law died too. Again, he was in need of money for the burial ceremony. So she went back to his friend the Pig and asked for another loan often bags of cowries. The Pig had pity on his friend and gave him the last ten bags of cowries that he had in his savings. The Pig begged the Tortoise to pay back the first loan in time to enable him go on a journey to buy food for his family. The Tortoise promised the Pig that he would abide by the terms of the loan.

Two months passed, the Tortoise could not raise the money as promised. He knew that the Pig would soon come, so the Tortoise decided to go on a journey. At the appointed time, the Pig went to meet the Tortoise.

"Where is my friend?" asked the Pig.

"He had gone on a journey to try to get some money to pay your debts", the Tortoise's wife replied. "He said you should wait for him however", she added.

The Pig thought his friend was honest. So he did not want to waste his time waiting for the Tortoise that day.

"Tell him I shall be back in two weeks", said the Pig.

Immediately the- Pig went away, the Tortoise returned home. His wife delivered his friend's message. Tortoise put his hands on his chest and thanked God that his friend had not assaulted to his wife. The problem however was still not solved. He had killed no animal to sell. In two weeks, his friend would still come back. The Tortoise then began to plan how he would avoid making his friend angry. He talked it over with his wife and both of them planned to play tricks on the Pig.

After two weeks, the Pig came back for the money."*

When the Tortoise saw him at a distance, he pretended to be beating his wife very seriously. The woman screamed for help. She begged her husband to stop beating her with the promise of repentance.

The Pig came in and found his friend's house in total confusion.

"Hey! What is the matter? He asked.

The Tortoise instead threatened to send his wife away from home. The Pig tried to intervene, but Tortoise would not give room for intervention.

"She has lost the money I gave her to keep to enable me clear my debts with you", the Tortoise told his friend. - "Now she has put me in shame", he added.

Full of pity, the Pig asked his friend to stop beating her. "I will allow you two more weeks to find the money", said the Pig. Tortoise thanked his friend very heartily for being so considerate. He promised to pay the Pig the debt in two weeks, and Pig went away. Two weeks is not a very long period and Tortoise had only one way of getting the money. He had to kill two or three animals and sell them. This depended on luck. What would happen if he cannot get the money? He devised another very serious strategy.

Two weeks passed and Tortoise had not killed any

animal and therefore had no money to pay back the Pig. On the day the Pig had to come for his money. Tortoise disguised to a grinding stone. He laid on his back and asked the wife to grind some pepper on his chest and the woman obeyed.

The Pig came and found the woman grinding pepper. He asked her where her husband was and she told him that he had gone behind the house and will be back shortly. She gave him a seat at a corner and Pig sat down. He waited indefinitely and Tortoise didn't show up. Pig had been sitting for four hours, a pretty long time for any busy person. Meanwhile Tortoise's wife continued grinding her pepper.

"Where on earth did you say your husband had gone to?" asked the Pig again, with a twist on his face.

"I said he had gone to the back of the house and will be back shortly", that she replied rudely. "lie has your money now and I will not be beaten this time as you caused me to be beaten two weeks ago. If you like, you can sit down and wait but if you don't like, you can go away"', added Tortoise's wife in an arrogant manner.

"The Pig got angry at this rude response and reflected on the incident that he had saved her from being ejected from her home two weeks earlier. He decided to teach her a lesson which he believed she would never forget. So the Pig seized the grinding stone that the woman was using and flung it far to the back of the house. The woman burst out crying because the supposed stone was her husband the Tortoise.

Suddenly, the Tortoise came in from the back of the house. "Why are you crying?"', he asked his wife.

"Look at your friend the Pig. IIe has flung my grinding stone behind the house".

The Pig tried to explain to Tortoise what had

happened but Tortoise would not listen. Rather, he told his friend the Pig that his money would be -paid if only Pig produces the exact grinding stone that was flung into the bush, to the back of the house.

The Pig foolishly went to the back of the house thinking that he would find the grinding stone he had flung in that direction. But he could not find the grinding stone. And till today, the Pig is still looking for that grinding stone.

That is why we always see the Pig digging everywhere, looking for the grinding stone.

Questions for Discussion
1. What other title can you suggest for this story?
2. What made the tortoise get into debt?
3. What was the first trick tortoise used to avoid paying Pig's debts?
4. Sin your opinion, do you think Pig realized that the grinding stone was Tortoise himself?
5. Do you think Tortoise should have paid his debt if Pig did not throw away his wife's grinding stone?
6. Was Tortoise really honest?
7. Explain these words: "intervention ", "strategy", "reflected"

THE SMALL DRUM

Once upon a time, all animals in the forest agreed to possess a drum each. There was a huge tree to be felled for that purpose. So anybody who succeeded in felling the tree won the price of getting the best section of it for his drum.

All powerful animals like the Lion, Elephant, Bushcow and Tiger were invited to the competition. After these animals had tried and failed, the Hare stepped into the scene. "Give me the chance to try too"! Demanded the Hare. The other animals laughed. That was a big joke.

"Where will you borrow the strength to fell a tree which has humiliated stronger and bigger animals?" the other animals asked?

Then Tiger drew Hare to a corner. "Do you think you are stronger that Elephant, Lion and myself?", Tiger asked. Hare gave deaf ears to these questions. After some consultation among themselves, all the animals decided to give Hare the axe as a challenge.

Very quickly, he collected the axe, and within a short time made big cuts into the trunk of the tree. And not long after the tree went crashing down with a deafening noise, pulling down smaller trees which surrounded it.

All the other animals were shocked and not long after the tree had fallen, the stronger animals immediately rushed to the scene and occupied the big sections of the tree trunk.

Poor Hare. He had no alternative but to select from the smaller branches. So he cut a small branch out of which he made a small pretty drum which produced a sharp pleasant tune.

To his advantage, none of those strong animals succeeded in making a good drum.

Early one morning, the animals heard hare play his small drum. It sounded melodious. So they all became jealous of the Hare and planned to seize the drum from the poor hare. But Hare was conscious of this wicked plan and so he decided to take refuge in a village which was situated across a river. His immediate problem was how to cross the river. He made several trips to the river bank looking for a means to cross the river.

One day, he discovered that he could cross through a hammock. So he stealthily crossed the river with his small drum.

Very early the next morning, the Hare played his drum, whose sound echoed through the entire forest. The other animals listened attentively but did not know from where the sound came. Hare continued playing his drum while the animals struggled to trace his whereabouts.

Eventually, they got to the bank of the river. Then one of them asked, "Hare, where are you?"

"1 am on this side of the river", replied the drum player.

"How can we join you? We have heard the pleasant tunes from your beautiful drum and would like to be with you", they added.

"I suggest you cross the river so as to help me carry my drum", he replied.

"But how do we do it?", they asked again.

"Use that instrument" he said, pointing to the hammock.

As the animals were determined to seize the drum from the Hare, they did not see the hammock as an obstacle. At once, they all got onto the hammock. When Hare saw that all the animals had climbed into the hammock, he used a sharp knife and cut off the hammock from his own end. Immediately, the hammock gave way, throwing all the animals into the river, where they were drowned.

""You reap what you sow", the hare shouted and went back into the village playing his small drum.

Questions for Discussion:
1. Suggest another title for this story
2. Who felt the tree and how was he rewarded?
3. Explain the meaning of "paid deaf ears to "
4. Narrate in your own words a situation where a strong person attempted to seize from a weak person what was his by right.
5. Explain the following words: "stealthily", "melodious", "deafening", and "obstacle".
The End

PART ONE B

THE IMAGE OF AN AFRICAN WOMAN IN THE FOLKTALE

The relationship between the folktale and culture has been long established and the folktale goes right back to the tribe. It is the vehicle through which a society's simplicity, beliefs and entire cultural practices are unveiled. For the purpose of this study, four tales have been selected:

• The Outcast who became master.
• The Wicked step mother
• The wicked mother
• Love at first sight

In all these stories, women are derided and rigidly categorized as cooks, baby sitters, mothers, house wives or romanticized as queens, goddesses or fairies, and lovers of wealth.

The representation in the tales is a direct reflection of women as perceived in our African society, a society where there is no question on who does what in the home. Every person grows up knowing that it is the woman who cooks the food, and generally sees to it that the house is clean and everything in the home is well done.

Like all human beings, women differ from one another in their temperaments and personal relationship with people in society. We see among Pa Tamfu's wives a difference between the first and second. The first wife was shrewd and cold while the second was kind and friendly with people in her locality.

Something worth noting is the acceptance of polygamy in the African society. As a tradition, when one woman dies or when she travels out of the home, the other takes over her responsibilities immediately. The responsibility of bringing up children is that of a woman. The man brings them to life but the child's sex and how they survive is not much of the father's problem.

Death is hardly taken for a natural phenomenon. It is often attributed to the hand of the devil and evil in the negative term - It is witchcraft. Just as we do not doubt the existence of witchcraft, or evil so too do we agree that there are people endowed with special powers that can reveal the devilish and mysterious acts of the devil in witchcraft. When these wizards are exposed, the offenders often take revenge.

In daily situations, women are ambitious and brave. The desire to attain greater heights often leads them to making heavy sacrifices that affect their families. Bih in the third tale, sacrifices her daughter to increase her tadpole catch.

The tales generally highlight a distinction between Man and Woman in the African traditional society. Woman is man's property because he pays a bride price for her, the amount differs from society to society and from family to family. He has right to marry as many times and as many women as he can. Man is the father, husband, leader, boss and he has the right to punish the woman if he so desires.

Consequently, he is often presented as being agile, aggressive and domineering. Woman on the other hand is made to play a submissive and productive role and she desires the love and respect from her husband only if she lives up to expectations.

Looking at the woman from a modern perspective, the African places her at a position that doesn't facilitate the design of a progressive agenda for her. Thanks to our policy makers who have designed an education

Programme with equal facilities for both sexes thereby emancipating the African woman. As literacy grows, the woman becomes fully emancipated.

THE OUTCAST WHO BECAME MASTER

There once lived a man called Pa Tamfu, in a far off town in the Grasslands. Pa Tamfu had two wives. The first had two children and she named her first child Willie and the second a female was named Martha. The second wife had an only son called Ekwaka.

The town woke one morning under a thick blanket of
rain. From the upper slopes of the hills came swirling pools of rain water. Because it had rained heavily for hours all night, so small brooks around the town got flooded and the climax of the days' events came when the death of Ekwaka's mother was announced. - ...

The entire neighbourhood was disturbed to get this news. Ekwaka's mother, was reticent, kind and tenderly to everyone. Who could visit that town without eating at her home? The entire town was depressed when the news of her death was confirmed.

Apart from recounting her contributions to the home, one thing disturbed her husband most. It was the thought of their son. 'Who will take care of my son?" he asked and cried all day. Ekwaka was still very young to take care of himself, he murmured.

"My first wife is not very friendly, she is harsh and shrewd. A woman of about forty with toughness and weariness on her face that suggested jealousy and hatred" Pa Tamfu was very depressed as he mourned for his second wife. Pa Tamfu had no sister who could render him that service and the thought of marrying another wife was still frightening.

And so one morning, he got Ekwaka by hand and handed him to his new mother. She could not turn down the offer. She received the tender hand in her usual shrewd manner, then dropped it down long before the husband finished what he was about to tell her. The indentation on her face betrayed that she stretched her arm to receive that of Ekwaka because the tradition compelled her to receive that orphan.

Pa Tamfu dropped his head gravely in agony but he could not help it. This first wife had been what she was all her life. He could therefore not change her over night. As an orphan, Ekwaka; s life depreciated fast. He had little to wear and to eat. His health was equally dwindling. His toes were infested with jiggers and eventually, he developed a lining of scabies on his body. House whole assignments were often accompanied with arrogance and facetious remarks. Often Ekwaka's stepmother would send him to the farm on an empty stomach under all weather to drive away birds from the young growing corn. Meanwhile, she stayed at home with her legitimate children giving them her motherly warmth. Only occasionally did her children go to the farm and they did so always after a good meal and during good weather. Every day, while the three children were at play, their mother would keep food in a room and cunningly sings her chorus.

Willie Willie come here
Willie Willie come here
Ekwaka Ekwaka stand there
Ekwaka Ekwaka stand there

This chorus was sung daily at mealtime and naturally only the children invited attended to the call while Ekwaka was instructed to 'stand there'. On arrival, their mother gave them the meal leaving her orphan hungry. Ekwaka grew pale with wrinkled eyelids, which gave him a frightful look. At the farm, he stayed under the sun for lone hours throwing stones at the birds. He closed the day late feeling hungry and worn out.

On return home, the stepmother gave him raw cocoyam or plantain and how and when he cooked the food was never her concern. Many a times, this food was given in a rude manner "Ekwaka! Ekwaka!" she would call.

"Mama! He replied in a depressed manner. "I know you will make your father feel that you are very hungry and nobody in this house cares about you except him". With a stern look, she instructed, "Pick up two plantains from the store to cook for yourself". Stealthily, he walked to the store, picked the plantains to boil for himself. His sauce was often pepper and salt.

Alter such dry meals, he often sat out in the shade to think over it.

One day, a little fairy visited Ekwaka in the farm. She found Ekwaka sitting on a stone with his head sunken deep into his laps. He had been weeping for long and his flabby eyes were an indication of his sorrow and paleness.

"Ekwaka!' she miraculously called. "Why are you crying? 'She asked. He raised up his head but he could not utter a word of reply.

The fairy had heard of Ekwaka's plights and so she came to see for herself.

"Ekwaka!" she again called. "Can I have that cocoyams?" She enquired. That was the only cocoyam that he had for the day as lunch. All the same, Ekwaka was generous and so he stretched his arm and surrendered the cocoyam to the unknown guest.

'This must be a kind child", the fairy thought, as she received the cocoyam. As soon as she received it from Ekwaka, she retired to a nook where she sang the chorus:

Willie Willie come here
Willie Willie come here
Ekwaka Ekwaka stand there
Ekwaka Ekwaka stand there

The children were familiar with the chorus and the outcome was obvious. In anticipation, Willie and Martha went very fast to their usual eating corner. But to their greatest shock the call that day had a different objective. Apparently, the fairy needed them for her meal. As such, she received them and killed them to use for her meal. When their mother returned from the market and called for them using their usual chorus, to her dismay no one appeared. She sang the chorus a second time but still, no body appeared. There was silence.

It was quite disturbing for her. So she walked up to her stepson to enquire on her children's whereabouts. Ekwaka paused for a while, then broke the news how the fairy visited them and later caught Willie and Martha for its meal. The woman dropped down in tears but she could not reverse the order of events. Her children were dead "and there could be no turning back. Initially, it was more like a dream but finally she learnt to accept it for something true.

She mourned in sackcloth and wore no hair. During that period of mourning, she was emotionally disturbed.

She had been used to the warmth of children, what she had lost when her children died. And so time and again, this problem disturbed her. One day, she went through her bedroom weeping and searching for the lost children. She turned through the rooms and back yard and saw no child except Ekwaka.

For a second, something spurred her to call Ekwaka to herself. Then she sat down to pull out all the jiggers from Ekwaka's feet gave him a good bath and fed him regularly.

With time, she found Ekwaka looking quite handsome and so the stepmother pulled Ekwaka to her bosom and she remained her favourite child till death.

Questions for discussions and written exercises

1. How many wives had Pa Tamfu? Describe theses wives.
2. Pa Tamfu must have been rich to marry two wives, yet he wasn't happy. What made him unhappy?
3. Ekwaka lost his mother at an early age. What circumstances made him a favourite child?

THE WICKED STEP-MOTHER

An orphan was once asked by the stepmother to wash plates in a fast running stream. The strong current suddenly swept away one bowl from his hands and carried it down stream. The orphan struggled to recover it but his efforts were abortive.

He placed his arms on his head and slowly and wearily, walked home crying. Immediately the stepmother saw him without the plate, she at once guessed what had happened. And so she at once broke in.

"I don't think you want to tell me that you have lost my plate?"

"Yes mama", he replied.

"What? You must be joking. You better go back to the stream and look for that bowl".

She was very furious. The miserable orphan bent his head downwards and started walking back to search for the bowl along the banks of the stream. He walked down stream for long. It seemed an awful long way from his starting point when suddenly he appeared at a hut in which he saw an old wretched woman. The orphan stood frozen, tired legs anchored in sand and anxious to go in to get shelter. This woman was astonished to see him, as a result she enquired, "What has brought you here, my son?"

"I have lost my step mother's plate and have been compelled to look for it if not I would be expelled from home", he replied.

"What! Expelled? Because of a plate? You make me develop goose skin "she remarked.

She pulled him to herself then later offered him a sit. His feet were cold and wet. As he stood, one could see on his countenance that he was not happy. The old woman though feeble, sympathized with the child.

"You will continue your journey tomorrow" she said while parting his back.

Earlier, the boy had looked at the hut with fear. It was quite old with broken walls and a wet floor. From a small barred window, too high to see though, came a week ray of the sun. In his trembling fear, he saw some food being cooked.

At last, there was some hope of having something to eat, he thought. And so despite these odds, the boy felt quite relaxed with the old woman.

The old woman was equally happy to receive such a nice boy. He woke up early every morning to assist this woman. He washed her plates and cleared off the entire dirt that was abandoned behind the hut. In return for his good gesture she wished she had a good meal to offer the boy. In the absence of anything better, she cooked plantain and served with the last bit of palm oil that she had. The boy enjoyed the meal and he didn't hide his feelings when he sincerely thanked her.

The next day, before the woman left for her farm, she asked the boy to guard the hut then warned him not to play with any girl who might come in, in her absence. It was however strange that, immediately the old woman left for her farm, a beautiful girl immerged and invited the boy to play with her. The boy was very busy repairing the old woman's hut and so he continued with his work.

"How are you?" the girl greeted.

"Fine" he replied but stopping to play would mean a drawback of his plan, because he gave priority to the repairs of the hut and gave a deaf car to the girl's invitation for play. The girl was highly disappointed and so reluctantly, she walked away.

When the old woman came home, she was very happy to see her hut looking better than before. She nodded in satisfaction but began wondering what she could give the boy as reward for his good work.

"You must be a very good boy" she expressed. "You must stay with me for some days" suggested the woman.

The boy gave thought to this suggestion^ then after some minutes, he shrugged his shoulders as he silently said

"Yes".

The boy's absence from his father's home did not disturb the stepmother at all. She was rather happy that a burden had been taken off her shoulders except for moments she thought of his daily chores.

When the boy settled down in obedience to^ the old woman's request, the old woman pointed to a hut opposite hers and said;

"Go into that hut, you will find bowls and eggs. To any that say, "don't take me", you take it and those that say "take me", you should not take them. When you finally arrive your home, clear a spot and crack the egg on that clear spot. The result will-be your reward for your kindness towards me".

The boy listened to the instructions attentively. Then he went into the hut and the bowl and egg that he took were those that said, 'don't take me'.

On arrival home, he did just what he was told by the old woman. He cleared the spot and on the cleared spot he cracked the egg. The outcome was a nice furnished house with all the riches on earth. The house was filled with music from an amplifier that made it more of a paradise of its own. It was not a big house though, but the flashlights on the four corners of the parlour threw so much brilliance down into the house that one could admire the furniture in the house. In the centre of the parlour, there was an Italian rug, trimmed with gold trimming made to match the curtains. The big lights moved, the music changed and everything in the house looked sweet and beautiful. In the garden, there was cattle, cars and real wealth. The Eldorado was owned by this simple and honest young man

The orphan's life style changed immediately. He now had a car, was rich and very popular. His nagging stepmother was amazed at her stepson's popularity.

"How has it happened that a child driven away for being careless has instead become great and popular?"

As an expression of jealousy she called up her son some day and said, "you lazy child, you only eat and play. Don't you see the fortune that your brother has brought by staying away from home for two days? Can't you imitate him by losing a similar bowl in that very stream?"

The boy went to bed that day with a heavy heart but determined to work hard and attain the same or higher goal.

Early the next morning he determined to take the challenge. He picked up all the dirty bowls in the house and took them to the stream for washing. Just before he left the house his mother had reminded him in a stern voice.

"I hope you will be wise enough to let lose one bowl in that stream".

"I have heard mama. I'll do so" the boy replied. When he got to the stream, he wilfully let lose a bowl into the water and watched it float down stream. Twigs and rocks obstructed the smooth float of the bowl but he got another twig and helped to push it down the stream. Then in pretence, he began to search for it

Apparently, he met the same old woman. The boy

however could not change his nature immediately. He was proud and snobbish. This woman was old and feeble. And so her sight was the first disturbing factor to every guest. Another factor that stroke any guest was her meals. Her food was fowl droppings and plantain peelings.

In his usual snobbish manner he could not stand the sight of that meal. When she served him this food, he shrugged his shoulders and in a cold manner he said, "We do not eat such dirty food in our home". The old woman listened to that remark, which left her cold, hearted though she managed to put on a cheerful face.

The nest day, she had to go to her farm. In her usual manner, she assigned the boy to help in repairing her roof and warned him from playing in case any girl called for a visit. She advised him not to give her a face. Contrary to the old woman's advice, at first sight, he fell in love with a beautiful girl who called at the hut, just when the old woman left for her farm. He played for too long with her and consequently, he could not do anything to help the old woman. Worst still on his part, the reckless play made him break the old woman's bed and stool.

When the old woman returned from her farm, she didn't feel happy to see her bed and stool broken

"You must have been playing I guess" she remarked.

"Of course mum. I am too young to stay without play" he replied. Mm... she grinned without saying any audible word. It was obvious that she would not stand that boy any longer.

Late that day, she sent the boy to the hut opposite hers with clear directives. "In that hut you will find big bowls and eggs telling you, "take me". Do not take them, she warned. As you continue in the hut, you will find small bowls and small eggs saying, "don't take me, don't take me". Those are the once that you should take" she advised.

With his usual arrogance and ambition reinforced by his mother's instructions, he didn't give the old woman's instructions a second thought and before he went round, he concluded that he will be a big fool if he does not pick up the big bowls and big eggs.

"Take me, take me' they repeated in high tones. Without wasting time, he went down and picked up the big bowl and big egg.

On arrival, he invited his intimate friends and relatives to help clear up the spot where he had to break the magic egg. His wicked and ambitious mother was too anxious to reap the outcome and so she pressed to sit right in front of the actor, the son.

While sitting in a very cosy chair at the centre of the crowd, she said beating her hand on her chest, "My son too has been to that stream and brought that special egg and bowl. He will soon break it and become the richest person in this land", she murmured nodding her head in joy.

She had planned a hectic reception for her son. After the lousy reception, the egg was cracked. News of the second magic egg had had gone far and wide. Hence the crowd that turned out to see the miraculous wealth was astonishing. Thousands of friends and relatives had been waiting for days each aiming at acquiring something from the booty.

Surprisingly, the reverse happened. Instead of wealth, pestilence and disease came out of the egg. There were snakes and wild animals ready to devour the boy, his mother and the waiting crowd. The diseases ranged from leprosy, epilepsy, madness and all bad diseases that we can think of. The boy's mother at once became a leper and all the other closed relatives and friends became invalids. In a short while, the boy and his family lost even that which they originally had and they lived in misery till death.

Questions for discussion and written exercises
1. What prompted the boy to go down stream?
2. Using the experience from this story, justify the fact that it pays to be kind and obedient, especially to the old.

THE WICKED MOTHER

In a certain isolated village, there lived a lady, her daughter and her friend. One day. this lady, her daughter and her friend went to fish tadpole. They took along baskets, nets and little cutlasses. The lady's friend caught a lot of tadpoles while the mother and child had just a bear catch. She struggled the whole day but still had just a few tadpoles. Late in the day,._ she expressed surprise at her misfortune then sought for advice from her friend.

"I have used my best baskets and applied the best - techniques yet I cannot catch the tadpoles. Occasionally, I had to thrust myself into the water in search of tadpoles that make their homes in the fissures of the rocks. Besides the baskets, we also have nets and cutlasses still aimed at facilitating the job but our efforts are all abortive. What advise can you give me?" She enquired.

"The solution to your problem is easy". The friend replied, "You need to make a sacrifice for this particular problem. You only need to push your daughter into the pool and you will have a good catch.

"Hmmm..." the lady murmured after listening to the suggestion. That will be great magic and society will credit me for taking home a lot of tadpoles.

In order to attain her goal, she pushed her daughter into the pool. Immediately, the child dropped into the hands of the mermaid who owns that pool, the ripples stretched out and the pool became clear, and from then on, her catch increased.

At the end of the fishing exercise, she had a basket full of tadpoles, but with mixed feelings. She packed the fish into a basket, which she placed on her head and walked home. Her journey home was not joyous, as she had earlier anticipated. As she journeyed through the tracks, she tried to pick out where her daughter may be, what she will tell her husband and the rest of the people in town.

Once she hit at a beehive hanging on a palm tree branch as she thrust through the bushes. The bees hummed angrily at her intrusion and tried to sting her but she brushed them off and walked on. The leaves rippled in the wind that blew from the riverbanks and the hollow stalks knocked against each other as the wind moved to and fro until she solemnly arrived home. Her husband didn't notice the absence of their daughter.

Late in the day, it occurred to him that he had not seen his daughter and so .he asked her whereabouts. "Mm....mm...." the mother murmured but said nothing and soon minutes passed for the father to forget. It was already getting dark and since the children usually sleep in their own rooms the father assumed that she had gone to sleep.

In the morning, the father saw the children very busy. Some were coming from the stream, others were sweeping his compound and the younger ones were by the fire side. Every, \ one of them greeted him but that particular daughter was not seen.

"Bih! Bih! Oh!", the man called on his wife. It's over a day since I saw my daughter, the one who accompanied you for fishing.

"Masa, I don't know what to tell u. it's true that I took my daughter to the stream for fishing. We went through the stream with her until we arrived at the point where the stream joins the main river. Eh....." Bih went silent in search of words. "What happened then with her?" the husband asked.

"She disappeared from the group and I have since not seen her myself she replied.

"You must be joking. And what did you do? Do you say that you continued fishing when you could not find your child?"

"Mmm" the mother murmured. With a scream, the father pulled into his room to think out what must have happened to his daughter.

Late that night, a wood cutter had gone to cut wood near the said tributary. He used his axe and just while he was cutting Kpo! Kpo! Kpo!, the supposed lost child came out of the pool and sat on a stone at the side of the pool and sang a solemn song:

Nchige Nkwi, mine-e-ching
Ukweli Ushwing nitiewre-ching
Megewa lege nivudibong-ching
Ndowa ma-a cham-a-ching
Mindinisane muofuobinwi-ching
Ndifana bas-ching
Ndi Ntswana ku-you-fuobinwi-ching
Translated to mean:
Charcoal fetcher - ching
Back home tell my father - ching
My mother is a bad woman — ching. She pushed
me into the pool - ching
I am now a baby sitter - ching
To the chief of gods - ching
Closing her doors - ching
And pounding her achu - ching.

The woodcutter on hearing this message stopped cutting to look at the singer more closely. Then she discovered that he was looking at her sternly, the mermaid mystically pulled her into the pool.

For a while, the woodcutter developed goose skin as

the pool tumbled. In a flash there was some lightening as the ripples stretched out from the pool. "Who must this be and what was she saying?" he murmured.

With a desperate effort, he regained courage to continue cutting his wood, Kpo! Kpo! Kpo! Again, the same girl came out and sang the same song. As she pronounced her last words, the woodcutter picked up his axe and walked off.

This must be the lost girl", he thought. "Something mysterious must have happened to her", he said to himself. He went home to convey the important message to the girl's father and the entire village.

When he reached the village, he narrated the story to the man who had lost his daughter then advised him to get traditional doctors to help him recover his daughter. Based on that advice, he invited two groups of doctors. The tall and the short doctors to assist him recover the girl from the pool. Before the traditional doctors moved to the pool, they had asked for a "heavy lunch. The father however gave' more meat to the tall doctors and less to the short doctors. The tall doctors didn't do as much as anticipated. They poured into the pool their charms and recited their rituals but they did not succeed to pull out the girl-

The short traditional doctors then took their turn. They dropped in a first charm followed by a second. Then they did - recite a few rituals invoking spirits to-help out the girl. These rituals appealed to the chief of the gods who miraculously released the girl. They brought her out and placed her on the stone for the father to identify. He was very satisfied with their performance but paralyzed when they dropped her back into the pool on grounds that he discriminated when he gave more meat to the tall doctors.

"Call on their height to bring out your daughter" they screamed. The girl's father pleaded for sympathy but the short doctors remained adamant. Then he called on friends and well wishers to help him with meat. The supply tripled what he had given to their counterparts. They ate and were quite satisfied. When the feasting was over, they pulled the girl from the pool and gave to the father. There was further feasting and merriment for many more days. The girl warned the mother to be watchful of the company that she keeps and the advise that she receives from her friends. Vaulting ambition has its many dangers.

Questions for Discussion and written exercises

1. Think out the things you often do or discuss with your friends. Working in groups of four, imagine problems that worry you and come up with solutions to these problems.
2. The girl's mother caught many tadpoles but she was still not happy. Why?
3. How did they recover the lost child?
4. What are the dangers of vaulting ambition?

LOVE AT FIRST SIGHT

In a far off country, there lived a very beautiful girl called Ongie. She had long hair, a fair complexion and a trimmed waistline. She was soft spoken and she walked elegantly with pride. When she laughed, she did so discretely. She was not one of the girls who would frequently visit drinking places for suitors.

When she discussed about marriage with her close friends, she will sometimes say, "I know I am beautiful and a cynosure of this land. Any person I will consider worthy will be my husband no matter what my parents say".

Some people tried to restrain her from making such remarks but still, she will not stop to reason with them.

Every man of rank who saw her fell in love with her.

Many suitors proposed marriage but she will always turn down the offer. News went far and wide about her and this disturbed her parents.

One day a boat constructor who had heard about her disguised himself as a handsome young man. For the moment he appeared more neatly than ever before. His hair and beard were trimmed and his clothes were quite smart such that he could make a find impression. Then he walked to the mirror and on seeing himself, he felt convinced that he could win the love of any beautiful woman on the land.

To carry out his mischievous plan, he acquired an apartment in a particular neighbourhood in the outskirts of the town. If he had to achieve his goal, he needed a few expensive and attractive articles of clothing. Hence, he borrowed a suit, shirt and tie from a rich neighbour who did not bother to know the particular occasion he was preparing for. However, it was his best suit and so he warned him to handle it with care.

From another neighbour he borrowed an elegant pair of shoes and a brief case. With the borrowed items, he felt very elated. He then took his time in putting on his borrowed robes.

"Yes", he said to himself while looking at a mirror. "I am the most handsome and richest young man in this land". Then he began to count the beautiful girls he had seen and to think out which of them he could court for marriage. He recollected that he had heard of a girl called Ongie who lived at the far end of the town. She is beautiful he heard, and so he decided to woe her for marriage.

"The men she refused are not handsome and they are old fashioned", he murmured. "I am handsome and my dress is cute and off the latest fashion. Besides that, I am sure that those men are not as rich as I am. Women love rich men" he concluded.

With that conviction, he went to visit Ongie. A distance away from Ongie's home, his handsomeness and attire caught Ongie's eyes. At first sight, she fell in love with him. She could not hide her feelings. She walked up to the man and asked if she could be of any help.

"Yes", he replied. My name is Bokwe. I am looking for the house of Miss eh...Ongie who lives in this part of the town".

"What name did you say that she is called?" Ongie asked to ascertain that she heard the right name. "Was it Ongie or Onie?,. she asked.

"I can't remember exactly" Bokwe pretended.

"I don't think that you mean Ongie", she said doubting.

"That is the name. Yes it is the name". Bokwe confirmed.

"Well, my name is Ongie. And if it is me that you are looking for, come in and take a seat". The young lady entreated Bokwe to a seat in her salon. "Before you tell us why you have come, what would you like to eat?" she asked.

"Anything", Bokwe replied. Ongie dug a kolanut from the verandah and served the guest. This was followed with a glass of water.

In the course of their conversation, Bokwe introduced the idea of marriage. The girl was elated.

"What a terrible coincidence, as if he could read her mind. She accepted the offer without hesitation and promised to tell her parents when they come home.

"But how soon will they come home?" he enquired. He was anxious to have the marriage contracted immediately because he had enough money on him for the bride price.

"Not very long dear, they should be in this evening", she replied. "If you come in at cock crow, you will surely meet them. I am equally anxious to go with you as your wife", she added.

After chatting on their fields of interest, the young man left but promised to call the next morning.

The girl's parents came in not long after the young man had left. She broke the news of having seen her long-awaited husband to her parents and she shocked them more[1] when she talked of going with him the next day. The parents however, didn't take her serious. They went to bed waiting to see that great man who could win their daughter's love in seconds.

At cockcrow, the well-dressed young man reappeared. Immediately, the girl heard a knock on the door, she rushed to open it.

"Just the person I had been expecting"', she said. She

embraced him and brought him to her parents and introduced him as her fiancé. The mother was puzzled at her daughter's behaviour and language. She did not hesitate to ask where and when she had known the man.

"Knowing the man, I knew him here yesterday", she replied.

"Ah!, that sounds strange, that you meet a man and decide to marry him the next day". She recounted her period of courtship with her husband and emphasized the importance of the two families knowing each other fairly well before the marriage". The idea of knowing each other well set the young man and lady laughing. To them, it was an old fashioned idea. Despite their laughter, the mother still explained to them that marriage in their land was a union of two families and for this union to be long lasting, it was necessary that both families understood each other fairly well before they embarked on the social contract.

Secondly, for any true marriage, it was expected that the two families come together to perform the necessary rites.

In view of these inadequacies, the girl's parents refused to give their consent to the marriage. But the girl and her young man could not tolerate those ideas. She wanted marriage and nothing more. In her view, it was not necessary for her parents to know her suitor's background neither was it necessary to get the two families involved.

She threatened to take away her life if her parents restrained her from going with the young man. All the talking by the parents did not change her at all. It was like throwing water on a duck's back.

"I must go, I must go with my husband"', she cried. In order to satisfy the two young and anxious persons, the girl's father asked the young man to pay the bride price. The old man with his wife by his side recalled the proverb, "If a child cries for huckleberry" (his wife cut in) "You give the child but if the huckleberry runs the child's bowels, you will not be blamed". This implies that they were prepared to give their daughter to her husband at her request and thereafter if anything arose, they were not to be blamed.

The suitor's briefcase was filled with new bank notes. He brought out millions of notes and spread them on a mat that laid in front of his would-be father - in - law. The old man nodded his head, with a dull face as he saw the young man arranging the notes in their various denominations.

In order to get the burden off his shoulders, he called on his little son, a younger brother to the girl to count the money and give it to his mother. When the little boy finished his assignment, he passed the money on to his mother who equally wore a long face. Nevertheless, she received the money.

Then she watched her husband yoke her daughter's right hand to her husband's hand and addressed them as husband and wife but reminded them of the slight on their tradition.

Before he uttered his words of blessings, he called for a cup of cold water which he poured on his daughter's feet while saying the proverb: "Though the cocoyam rots, let the seed remain to produce more cocoyams". This paraphrased his wish that before the daughter dies, she should leave behind children who would remain to continue the process of procreation. In conclusion, he advised them to travel to their home when they thought it necessary.

They thanked him for the ceremony and promised to

start off immediately after lunch. Immediately after lunch, they set out for their home, with no escort for the girl. This was another deviation from the girl's tribal tradition. The journey to the young man's home was tedious. But where there's a will, there's a way. The girl cheerfully made it. They reached their town late at night, when almost everybody had gone to sleep.

Because she was too tired, she went to bed immediately. But just before they fell asleep, they heard a tap at their door. The husband came out of bed to open the door. It was his neighbour from whom he borrowed a suit. He had come to collect it. The husband walked on tip toe into his bedroom to pick up the suit before his wife could notice. He handed it to the owner, while whispering his words of thanks.

When, he returned to bed, his wife inquired who that was but he immediately made up a story to convince her. They both went back to sleep but were woken up twice before midnight by neighbours who came to reclaim the shoe and brief case respectively. When they tapped at the door, in his usual polite manner he asked the wife to stay in bed and on return, he always had a well made up story to tell her. On the occasion when he handed out the briefcase, he wisely told his wife that the receiver was his friend who needed the case for a journey. The wife accepted the excuse with doubts because she recollected that she had seen him give out many things that he had at their marriage.

At that juncture, she began to suspect the person she had selected for a husband. But that of course was not the only strange thing that she would se.

Before the cock crew, the being that slept in front of her as husband had changed to something else. The head was that of a serpent while the feet were still human.

She gazed at it with surprise, but was still not convinced that what her eyes saw was the image she had in mind. She got up and opened the window to get light, but that creature grabbed her from the feet and in the struggle to swallow her up, it finally went back to itself: a boa constrictor. Neighbours who came in the next morning to greet the new wife found the girl's head still sprouting out as she uttered her last words of regret in tears. The tragedy explains why young people must take the advice of adults in the choice of their partners.

Questions for Discussion and written exercises

1. What presentations did the disguised Boa Constrictor make before he met the beautiful girl?
2. Why did the girl's decision to marry the handsome young man shock her parents?
3. How did the young man and woman react to the mother's advice?
4. Describe any marriage ceremony that you have witnessed,
5. Write out an imaginary monologue by the girl when she discovered that she was lying in bed with a creature whose head was a serpent and its feet human.
6. Say how marriage is conducted in your own tribe or area.
7. Here is a libation recital at a Cameroonian marriage feast. Read it and answer the questions that follow:

Father of our ancestors
Friends in our midst
We your children gather here
To send off our daughter in marriage
Here is your food (he drops the food)
Here is your drink (he drops the drink)

We pray on you to invite
Your long departed brothers and sisters
To join in this feast
Which to us is a joyous occasion.
Father of our ancestors
Friends of us all
We call on you to join us
In sending off our daughter in marriage
Grant her that gift of fertility
And call on your departed brothers and sisters
To wish her joy and happiness
In the same manner that we here on earth do wish her
Grant her wealth in food
Grant her peace in mind
And grant all gathered here the love of one another
Peace be to you all.

a) What occasion calls for libation in your tribe?
b) Do you find anything similar or different in the beliefs of your Christian church and those of this African tribe? Discuss the similarities and differences.
c) Name four things that an African family would wish their daughter escorted to marriage to own.

PART TWO

RIDDLES

1. I have a pond that never dries up no matter how much water you drain out of it
2. A pond with only one fish inside
3. My father and I went on a journey. When we arrived at our destination, he entered the house leaving me outside
4. I build my house without a door
5. He wears a hat in the forest
6. I see you but you cannot see me
7. I prepare a pot of vegetables each month which serves the whole world
8. I am a hunter. I kill the deer but bring home only the blood
9. A small animal without blood
10. I go everywhere with my house
11. You cannot climb us
12. A young lady with her long neck lives in a farm.
13. The bag which my father gave me can never be opened.
14. I go alone, but return with many more of my specie
15. I have a friend who goes everywhere with me but leaves only when I am asleep.
16. He touches the chief's head without fear.
17. I dress well in the farm but when brought home. I am naked.
18. In our father's palace, each person lives in his own room
19. He is a blind man but he can catch animals.
20. Only three of us can carry the king
21. Two sons of the king are fighting for the throne.
22. The king's stony farm.
23. 1 am one who has no legs but I walk and climb trees.
24. When I passed here you saw me but when I went

back, you did not see me.

25 1 converse while going to the stream but become silent on my way home.

26. My fence is built by God.

27. A small river that flows when it is angry.

28. I was born with chicken-pox and will die with chicken pox.

29. A small man with a hat.

30. A small house with many occupants.

31. I am in and out of the house.

32. I am there but nobody sees me.

33. A chief's wife with bells.

34. I have a child who wears a new dress daily.

35. You cannot count us.

36. A sea with only one fish and many crabs.

37. I was born with a coat on.

38. Two brothers living in the same house but cannot see each other.

39. We tie and carry the bundle without knowing the content.

40. We move in lines.

41. We fall without a sound.

42. My sister and 1 live in the same quarters but we never visit each other.

43. We were born on the same day but my friend is bigger than I.

44. He has a house but never knows it.

45. Two pieces of wood can cook an elephant.

46. I am a glutton, I eat but never have my fill.

47. I build a roof with one central pole. '

48. I have a glowing fire that never burns.

49. It travels though it has no legs.

50. Both of us are rulers, one reigns at night and the other in the day.

51. They beat drums at the back of your mother's house.
52. I am a strong soldier who can destroy a city in a short time but my greatest enemy is water.
53. I live both on land and in water.
54. I have a debt that must be paid some day, but I do not know when.
55. I am three times taller in the morning than in the evening. Who am I?
56. If fire burns in my stomach, what am I?
57. I always accompany you, yet I am not part of you.
58. I keep my cattle in its stable but its tail remains outside.
59. All the women are dancing in the King's company.
60. Two people are under the rain, one is exposed to the rain and the other remains unexposed.
61. I have a dress but I do not know what it looks like.
62. There are many of us in our house but we cannot deter mine one another's sex.
63. Soldiers on the road.
64. A walking stick lying on the road.
65. A creature that invites its own death.
66. A soldier in the soil.
67. 1 am caught in water and cooked in water.
68. On arrival I put on a red dress, on departure, I put on a black dress. What am I?
69. My child is seen everywhere.
70. Two soldiers who fight in a war.
71. You and I are related, yet we hate ourselves.
72. A two-headed snake.
73. I am always before you, though you cannot see me.
74. The one laughs, the other weeps.
75.1 have no legs and I cannot move, but I can run up and down mountains, across places, villages, towns, and cities. Who am I?

76. In the morning I walk on four legs. At noon I walk on two legs and in the evening, I walk on three legs. Who am I?

77. On the way-to the farm, I am the last. On the return trip I am the last also. Who am I?

78. A rich man with one nostril.

79. The cow says she's angry. Why?

80. There's a pool where everybody swims only at the edge.

81. What is it that invites death to take him?

82. A man who wears a white coat and a yellow skirt.

ANSWERS TO RIDDLES

Experience has shown that answers to riddles are greatly related to the environment. It is therefore necessary that after reading a certain number of riddles, children should be asked to suggest other possible answers in relation to their background. They should also be asked to translate their riddles from their mother tongues, into English so as to bring out the correct themes and answers.

1. The mouth: it never gets dry of saliva.
2. The tongue in the mouth
3. A walking stick
4. An egg
5. An ant hill
6. A child in the womb
7. Moonlight
8. The palm wine tapper: he brings home the wine, leaving the palm tree in the bush
9. A snail
10. A snail, tortoise, turtle
11 Rain drops, the blade of a knife, cutlass
12. The cocoyam flower
13. The contents of the stomach cannot be seen
14. A kernel
15. My shadow
16. A blade
17. A cob of maize when harvested
18. Pepper
19. A trap
20. The three stones that supports a cooking pot
21. Your two legs, each racing to arrive first as you walk
22. The sky and its stars
23. A snake
24. The sun

25. When which rattles when empty but makes no sound when filled with water
26. The teeth surrounding the tongue
27. Tears that run down the eyes in sorrow
28. Pineapple
29. Mushroom
30. Bee hive or anthill
31. Door, walls
32. Air
33. Sugarcane leaves
34. Stomach: taking food daily
35. Rain drops, hair strands etc which cannot be counted
36. The mouth with the tongue and the teeth
37. Cricket
38. Two eyes both on the head but cannot see each other
39. Pregnancy
40. Ants
41. A lady's breast
42. Walls of a house standing apart
43. The index and thumb finger
44. The dead does not know his grave
45. Two breasts do feed a state leader
46. The earth which takes the dead but never has its fill
47. Mushroom
48. The moon
49. The wind
50. The moon and the sun
51. Rain drops on plantain or cocoyam leaves
52. Fire
53. A crab, a crocodile, a frog
54. Death: because no one knows the day of the death
55. Shadow

56. Lamp: as a container of fire
57. Shadow-
58. Smoke: for it trails out of the house
59. Rain drops
60. Pregnant woman: the child in the womb not exposed to the rain
61. A child in the womb: no one knows what it looks like
62. When a hen lays eggs, it cannot determine which sex each egg will produce when hatched -
63. Ants
64. A snake
65. Cricket: when it cries
66. An ant
67. Fish
68. Plum: it is red when unripe and black when ripe.
69. The moon.
70. Eyes: rolling in their sockets
71. The dry and rainy seasons
72. A bridge
73. The face
74. The ripe and the unripe palm cones and their positions
75. A road
76. An old man: creeps with the knees and hands when a baby, walks on two legs as an adult and uses a walking stick to help him walk when very old.
77. The heels of our feet
78. A gun
79. Because the goat which is smaller can give birth to more than one young goat while the cow with its size can only give birth to one young one at a time.
80. Fire: everybody basks only at its edge.
81. Cricket—the sound it makes invites people to kill it

82. An egg: t shell is white and the yoke is yellow

PART THREE

THOUGHTS THROUGH PROVERBS

<u>**Definition of Proverb:**</u>
Various definitions of a proverb have been advanced but it seems that none of the* definitions has satisfactorily silenced criticism. Perhaps it is safe to say that there are as many definitions as there are paraomographers or writers on proverbs. Everyone seems to know what it is but none is able to provide a concise and complete definition that will silence criticism.

However, writers on proverbs have successfully explained what the proverb is, not by any internally consistent and accurate definitions but identifying some dominant characteristics that usually constitute a true proverb.

Some definitions place emphasis on brevity, some on form, some on content, some on popularity and some on role but any attempt to combine all these elements in a single definition is likely to result to wordiness and thus incomprehension and further criticism. For the purpose of this study, the researcher will contend herself with the following definition from the Longman Larousse dictionary, which states thus: "A brief familiar maxim of folk wisdom, usually compressed in form, often involving a bold image and frequently a jingle that catches the memory".

The Swedish definition may perhaps be easier: "A proverb is what man thinks". In simple terms, a proverb is a selection of words put into sentences from detailed observation of behaviour of human beings, animals, plants, natural phenomena, folklore, beliefs, attitudes, perceptions, emotions and the entire system of thoughts. No wonder Durkheim called proverbs, "Les representations collectives" of the society.

To understand and appreciate proverbs, one needs to be immersed in the speech environment that articulates a collective defined tradition with fixed expressions that constitute the linguistic core of the people.

Why Study Proverbs?
The question could be put the other way round. Why did the researcher study these proverbs?

Collecting these proverbs for this booklet was both fun and educational. The study started with a recording of one hundred proverbs from the researcher's background in Manyu Division. Initially, it was an eye opener to the Manyu culture, and then later it became a tool to teaching/ learning moral lessons.

It took slightly over three months to collect these proverbs. Then I moved on to interpreting the proverbs through consultations with people of my background and other tribes. The interpretations and variants were recorded and they unfolded the fact that proverbs have had a subtle and pervasive influence on popular opinion and are also very trustworthy witnesses to the social, political, ethical and moral ideas of a people among whom they originate and circulate.

On the significance of the proverbs, Gerber, quoted by Kelso, observes that it is very significant in its influence on the formation and preservation of the modes of thought and that its influence on the civilization of nations is exceedingly far-reaching.

In the ancient times, the use of proverbs was wide spread and its influence on the. civilization of nations is exceedingly far-reaching. Solomon's book of proverbs in the scriptures is a good example. The living Bible paraphrases it thus: "He (Solomon) wrote them to teach his people how to live and how to act in every circumstance (1:2). Proverbs are all about wisdom for living.

By bringing out the themes highlighted in the proverbs in this collection, one inevitably brings out the people's psyche and behavioural patterns. This is because proverbs may serve as an unwritten testimony of a people. They express the people's view as they may be, on life and how human beings of all sorts live in it, on God, and the world, good fortune and bad fortune as well as youth and old age.

In spite of the fact that this collection is not a comparative study of Cameroonian proverbs, the striking similarities that were discovered between proverbs in Manyu Division and those of the other, and languages are fascinating and, consequently, enhance the concept of Universality of proverbs. You take the example of the proverb, "When your brother is on the plum tree, you are sure of the ripe one" another variant reads: "When your brother is on the mango tree, you are sure of a ripe one". This proverb runs across most tribes in Cameroon and the meaning is the same. The foreign variants to our Cameroonian proverbs equally unveil similarities in-our thinking, even though they originate in different backgrounds. What does that portray? The answer is that, we are one, irrespective of colour or tribe. Mankind is the same and reasons alike. Their different environments create the differences in human beings. Through the use of proverbs, we express the variety of mankind and the universality of our emotions, thoughts and problems.

In the past, proverbs were a useful tool in the socialization of the youth. Socialization involves the inculcation in our off spring the norms, beliefs, values and practices of the society

The traditional Cameroonian child before the introduction of formal education, passed through four or five stages of a life cycle, to be accepted as a man or woman in his society. The stages were, birth, initiation, marriage, title taking and death.

Among the Manyu tribes for instance, tradition required that every child after birth had a period of initiation and moral upbringing before he could be given a place in the adult cycle. Young men who had not been initiated into 'Ekpe' society for instance, will never sit down while drinking in a gathering with adult men.

Morally, there was the emphasis on respect for parents, elders and defaulters were severely punished. There was equal emphasis on correct sexual behaviour, honesty, patience, obedience, unity, responsibility, humility and similar virtues.

The main vehicle for transmitting these values was through our oral literature such as folktales, riddles, folklore and proverbs.

Proverbs, Okpe argues, "Offer lessons of conduct on a day to day basis, the kind of education that the citizens of a society need to get along in their ordinary lives. We have to turn to proverbs and to fables that are exchanged in the moonlit family compound. Proverbs are themselves told in all sorts of situations during conversations, within stories etc. and serve a variety of purpose. Proverbs teach us about human nature and the way we think."

Thus, during each of the five stages of the journey through life, there is traditionally a ritual observance which is put in oral literature of some kind or the other. For instance, a newly born child is greeted with specific songs just as adolescents are instructed through specific folktales and proverbs, how to respect each sex and responsibility in the community. Before a child is installed or a title is offered, he/she is put under exclusion for some time to receive some moral instruction, which will guide him in his daily contacts with his subjects.

The last stage in one's life being death is an occasion generally accompanied by a sense of sorrow, but it is very important and people react to it differently depending on some factors such as the deceased's status in society, age, profession or cult affiliation. To die in dignity is to experience victory over life. To die without proper ceremonies, without the entourage of other human beings is interpreted to mean a life not well spent and the possibility of the disease maintaining a distant relationship with God. This explains why people spend exorbitantly on funeral rites religious or non-religious.

Our youths need to be instructed on the norms of conduct, customs, beliefs and practices of society, and proverbs do play a great role in providing these lessons.

Proverbs like fables have a message for the listener. They are intended to pass on the core and modality of the local culture to the younger generations. This can be seen in the proverb that says, "The hand that goes to the anus often, will someday touch faeces."

Some proverbs are couched in questions to make them sound gentler e.g. "Does the Leopard mourn for its lost cub?" Can the hand wash itself?"

From personal experience, I know how effective this could be in correcting one who does not want to share or is too self-centred. The proverb, 'Can the hand wash itself dawns on us that collaboration with one another for survival helps.

Proverbs can also be used as consolation for someone who is suffering. Take a situation where you and an adult or a stronger person seizing from a younger or weak person some property, you intervene and tell the older person that "The hen is never small when brooding on its egg". The message - giving respect to one who owns a thing will be got at once.

In most African societies, proverbs are often played on drums, included in songs, epics and folktales. In several West African cultures, once literacy skill is measured by the fluency with which one can use proverbs to express his experiences. The best statement on the value of proverbs in the African speech comes from the great African novelist - Chinua Achebe who describes them in his novel "Things Fall Apart" (1959) as the palm oil with which words are eaten.

Our collection has been presented bearing in mind the following themes - gossip, patience, unity, marriage, humility etc.

In conclusion, this study has attempted to bring out over one hundred proverbs with their variants and interpretations. Through the interpretations, one sees how the proverbs are used as a means to socialize in the Cameroonian tribes under study - Ejahgam, Mbo, Bali, Banyangi, Bakweri, Douala just to mention a few.

The proverb is one of the genres of folklore, which can be used as a strong vehicle in the transmission of moral values. Thus, the similarities in meanings enhance the concept of universality of proverbs and thoughts. A close study of the proverbs marked with asterisks establishes the fact that Cameroonian proverbs are a source of moral education.

Consequently, the proverbs, even though few, should provide useful material to unite us as students in colleges, provide language for Dramatists, Musicians, Politicians, Educationist, Orators and Preachers. We hope that as you read the proverbs and their interpretations, you will search through your own language to get it or its variant.

For the convenience of readers, these proverbs have been recorded, guided by key words, which are placed in alphabetical order.

May you enjoy browsing through the proverbs as much as I have enjoyed collecting and interpreting them.

PROVERBS

A as in Ant, Ash, Anus, Age mate.

**1. The ant does not cross a stream without a trail.
(Kenyang, Ejahgam, Nweh)**
Reliance on something or somebody to solve a problem or achieve something;

**2. If you stoop down to observe someone
else's anus, you expose your own anus to
some other persons.
(Ejahgam, Nweh, Kenyang)**
Another variant is: if you gossip someone's child, someday another person will gossip your own child. - The English variant is 'you reap what you sow."

**3. The hand that goes to the anus often, will
someday touch faeces.
(Bah, Nso, Kenyang, Ejahgam, Wimbum)**
If you do not break a bad habit early enough, you will reap dangerous consequences.
The English .variant is, "Too much of a thing is a disease"

**4. It is better to condole with your age mate
when he is bereaved than to condole with his
son when he (the age mate) dies.
(Kenyang, Ejahgam)**
(There is emphasis on age and age groups. Age mates know themselves fairly well.) Thus the proverb means that:
It is better to deal with one whom you know so well, than one you do not know.

The English variant is: 'It is better to deal with the devil you know than the angel that you do not know.'

5. No animal gives birth to an animal of a different species.
  (Lamnso)
  He shall reap hemp, who sows hemp and beans who sows beans.
  Chinese variant is: 'You reap what you sow.'

6. Ashes fly back in the face of the thrower.
(Menda-Nkwe)
  Reaping what you sow. If you plan evil, you will reap evil.
  B as in Bat, Baby, Bees, Birds, Blind man, Bitter leaf.

7. The bat knows that it is ugly and so it flies in the night.
  (Wimbum)
  The Krio variant is: 'Know yourself no bi kosh.'
  If you know your strength and weaknesses, it saves you from a lot of embarrassment.

8. When running away from bees, throw away the honeycomb.
  (Wimbum)
If you have a problem with someone, make sure that you do not owe him.

9. All birds cannot reach the sky.
(Wimbum and all Manyu tribes)
  Not all persons can attain certain heights.

10. The blind man vows to remain friendly with his

neighbours but his walking stick gets him into problems with his neighbour's calabash
(Kenyang)

One living with a large family cannot vow to live without problems in his neighbourhood. He may avoid the problem but his kin will not.

11. The baby in the womb delays her birth so as to kill the mother but she fails to know that if her mother dies in pregnancy, she also dies with her. (Kenyang, Bakweri, Nweh)

If you create problems for people at close quarters, you too will not have peace of mind.

The Wimbum variant is: A child who decides -that the mother will not rest, he will not also rest.

12. If you have not touched bitter leaf, you will not have bitter hands.

(Most languages in Cameroon)

Though the sword of justice be sharp, it will not slay the innocent.

The Chinese variant is: The law does not punish the innocent persons.

13. The noisy parrot does not eat a ripe plum. (Kenyang, Ejahgam)

The noisy bird does not build a nest.

Kenyang, Bakweri and Bum variant: A clock bird hardly builds a nest.

The English variant: 'Empty vessels make the loudest noise.'

14. If you are unable to reach the higher barn, you can at least reach the lower one.

(Kenyang, Ejahgam)

If you are unable to reach a higher wrung, you willingly exert your authority and position on the lower one.

15. The woodpecker promised to hew the mother's grave on a rock. The day the mother died, he nursed a boil on its beak.
(Kenyang, Ejahgam)

You may have the ambition to do a thing but you find that you cannot do It when it is due because something just abruptly befalls you and make it impossible for you to achieve your goal

C as in Cat, Children, Cock, Cow, Crab, Cocoyam.

16. The cat hides at nooks so as to eat fresh meat
(Kenyang) Patience is rewarding.

The English variant is: 'A patient dog eats the fattest bone.'

Buganda variant: The one who lies in ambush long enough is assured of catching juicy meat.

17. A cock does not crow on foreign land.
(Kenyang, Bakossi, Bakweri)

A stranger has no power on foreign ground.

Thonga variant: The strength of the crocodile is seen only in water.

18. Can you deny a crab water?
(Kenyang)

Wimbum variant: Can a crab beg for water from a bectle?

English variant is: Carrying coals to Newcastle.

19. Hate the cow and drink from its horns.
(Wimbum)
Hate a man and love his children.

20. Cow weh i no get tail na God di drive am fly.
(Pidgin)
God protects a person who does not have any one to take care of him.

21. Who knows a King at birth?
(Kenyang, Ejahgam)
The future is bleak. A baby today may be a great person tomorrow, as a result we are advised to be nice to children.

22. A child does not fall from a doorstep twice.
(Kenyang, Ejahgam)
English variant is: Once beaten, twice shy.
German variant: He who has burnt his tongue does not forget to blow on the soup.

23. A weak child sets his mother always fighting with neighbours.
(Kenyang)
(The, average African mother advises her child to fight back when attacked by an enemy. Where the child is a weakling, the mother has to continually intervene in defence of her child.)
The proverb therefore means that: "A weak child hardly gains his independence. He is always depending on the parents to survive.

24. It takes a village a village to raise a child.
(Mbo)

In Africa, child rearing is not solely the responsibility of the parents. The responsibility is shared by the entire village. The child is yours when he is in the womb but once born, he is for the society.

25. Two or more calabashes must rattle when put together.
(Kenyang, Bakweri)

It is normal for two or more people put together to interact or quarrel.

26. The living chicken learns from the dead one.
(Wimbum)

You learn from other people's pit falls.

27. If a child excretes on your thigh, you cannot amputate it.
(Kenyang, Ejahgam)

If a child touches excrement, you can only wipe it but cannot cut off its hands.

(If the one that you love or one with whom you are biologically related offends you, you cannot change the biological relationship. Thus there is need for forgiveness.)

28. The cocoyam seed rots but the sucker survives so as to yield more cocoyams.
(Kenyang, Bakweri)

When the old die, they should leave behind the young to procreate. (A wish)

D as in Dog, as in Drinks

29. When two dogs are fighting for a bone, take it away.
(Wimbum)
Whenever there is a problem, treat the cause in order to solve it.

30. A dog feels the hearth with its claws before it lies on it.
(Bafut)
The English variant is: **"Look** before you leap"

31. When you call a dog, do not hold a cane.
(Menda-Nken, Kenyang, Bakweri)
Do not invite one while keeping something that will scare him away.

32. He who serves drinks is always blamed.
(Kenyang, Ejahgam)
The person who serves palm wine is expected to know the status and rank of every person present and to serve them accordingly. He may go wrong since drinking houses are often open to all. The proverb means that, 'He who is exposed to the public must expect criticism especially leaders'

E as in Eye, Elephant, Eru, Excrete.

33. The eye never catches an animal.
(Kijem, Kenyang, Pidgin)
What you dream may not be realized until you work for it.

34. When the eye has a problem, the nose is affected.
(Wimbum)

All the parts of the whole get affected when one person has a problem.

35. No eye can see the chin.
(Bakweri)

This proverb is used to adjust morality. It is like saying that, the eye that sees, sees not itself.

36. If the elephant is defeated, what more of the Hare?
(Bakweri)

If the Mbu River fails to drown me, can the stream around do it?

Bakossi variant: If the greater/stronger persons are put off, what more the weaker ones?

37. If you take shelter in a hut, do not excrete in it.
(Wimbum)

If you receive help from a source, do not block the chances for others.

38. If the Eru is yours, you will pound it if you cannot chop it.
(Kenyang, Ejahgam)

Eru is a vegetable that has to be skilfully chopped before cooking. If you cannot however chop it, you should pound it.

Make appropriate use of what nature has given you.

39. When two elephants fight, it is the grass and trees that bear the pain of the fight.
(Mbo, Kenyang, Ejahgam)

When there is violence in a house for instance between the husband and the wife, the children suffer. When there is violence between leaders, the subjects suffer.

The Swahili variant is: The elephants quarrelled and the grass was crushed.'

F as in Farm, Feathers, Finger, Files, Firewood, Fon, Funeral.

40. No one makes a single farm against the rainy season.
(Bakweri)

A single investment is not enough for an ambitious person.

41. Good feathers do not necessarily make a good bird.
(Bakossi)

The English variants being:
Not all that glitters is gold.
The face is no index to the heart
There is no act to find the mind's construction in the face (Shakespeare in Macbeth)

42. The finger that brings out larvae from the palm tree must be flexible and soft.
(Bakossi, Kenyang)

In searching for something valuable, you must be soft and friendly.

43. Firewood that had been partly burnt lights

easily when put on fire.
(Kenyang, Ejahgam)
Old friends easily renew their links when they meet.

44. All fingers are not the same.
(Kenyang)
Things made the same are not necessarily the same.

45. An unfortunate man's hunting dog will only catch lizards.
(Ejahgam)
With ill luck, nothing good comes your way.

46. We do not put off fire by using dry palm fronds.
(Wimbum)
You do not suppress tension by using words that may aggravate the situation.

47. If you make a glowing fire, you must like smoke.
(Nweh)
If you take the fire stock, you have also taken along smoke.

Bakweri variant: Things that go jointly must be accepted jointly.

48. Whosoever chooses to take the intestine of an animal must be ready to handle the waste matter.
(Kenyang, Mbo)
Another variant is: "Those who want rain must also accept the mud that comes with the rain."

One who is ready to partake in an act must also be ready to bear the consequences.

To every enjoyable experience, there is a price.

49. A spark of fire can burn the whole bush.
(Nweh)

A little gossip can destroy a nation or group. Words are dynamite. They can destroy people if used wrongly.

Proverbs 16:28 says, "A perverse man stirs up dissention and a gossip separates close friends.

Proverbs 25:23 says, "and a gossip brings anger just as surely as the north wind brings rain.

Proverbs 26:20 says, "Without wood, a fire goes out; without gossip, a quarrel dies down.

50. If you hate flies, do not nurse an open wound.
(Kenyang, Nweh)

If you hate a thing, do not cohabit a situation that will attract it.

51. He who defecates on his way will meet flies on his return.
(Kenyang)

The English variant is: "Reaping what you sow."

52. You cannot attend one's funeral when he is alive.
(Kenyang)

You cannot represent one when he is present.

53. One finger cannot pick up a louse
(Nweh, Ejahgam, Bakweri, Wimbum)

One tree cannot make a forest

One hand cannot tie a knot

You need the company of some other person to accomplish a certain task. Unity is strength, the benefits of joint action. (In Africa, the individual lives for the community and the community in turn serves the individual.)

Many hands make a difficult job seem easy.

54. The housefly does not associate with a broom.
(Kenyang, Ejahgam)

Living things seek their level and they maintain it either instinctively or guardedly. Consequently, the fly does not associate with the broom because the broom would kill it. Once there is insecurity, we cannot expect unity.

55. The Fon or juju sees with his occiput.
(Anwi)

The words 'Ton or juju' refer to the state. The state is made up of people and whatever you do, the state with its many eyes can see.

56. That fruit which is ripe will fall off at its own accord.
(Mho, Bakweri)

There is time for everything. No one tells a baby that it is time to be born or does anyone tell another person when to die. We take our natural position in the flow of life.

(See Ecclesiastes 3: 1-15)

G as in Goat, Game

57. If you want the nanny goat catch the kid.
(Kenyang)

If you want a thing, use the right bait to get it.

58. The baby goat eats the same leaf with its nanny.
(Kenyang)
The English variant is: "Like mother like child"
See Proverb 22:6 "Can a good parent produce a bad child?"

59. If a goat is not fatty, you must make up with a calabash of oil.
(Kenyang)
Compensating for the inadequacies in life.

60. A dead goat should compensate for a fat and healthy one
(Kenyang)
Demanding payment for an inferior good.

61. The game does not fear the gun.
(Kenyang)
Wimbum variant is: The corpse does not fear the coffin.
Bakweri variant: The corpse never fears to rot.
What cannot be avoided must be endured.

62. An unloaded gun cannot be taken to war.
(Bakweri)
You cannot successfully perform a task without the necessary tools.

H as in Hurry, Hand, Humility, Hen, House, Hut, Haste.
63. Hurry, hurry, breaks the trouser
(Pidgin)
Patience is the key to all the good things

Tanzania variant: The impatient man eats raw food.
Swahili variant: The patient man eats ripe fruits.

64. Can the hand wash itself?
(Kenyang, Ejahgam, Esu)
One hand cannot tie a bundle.
Many hands do light work.
(The proverb brings out the importance of
collaboration, with one another for survival.)

65. If a servant washes his hands clean, he wines and dines with kings and queens.
(Nkambe)
If a junior or lower person is submissive, he would be
elevated to the rank and status of his masters. Humility
is rewarding.

66. The hand comes in as it goes out.
(Kom)
As much as you give so shall you receive. (This is in
line with Christian doctrine of- "The more you give, the
more you receive.)

67. They always insult the leader (Fon, Chief)
(Kom, Kenyang)
Bakweri variant: The face has respect but the back is
always abused.
(The Fon, Chief or any leader is the highest authority
in the land. Though he has weaknesses in discharging
his duties, it is better criticizing him in his absence so as
to ensure respect for institutions that rule the land.)

68. A ruler's head must be porous.
(Lamnso)

One called to administer must be prepared to hear much but should be capable of screening and selecting what will foster the growth of his institution.

69. A big head must accept nocks
(Kenyang)
One called to administer must accept criticism.

70. A hen is never small when brooding on its eggs.
(Ejahgam, Kenyang)
One is never small over his/her property.

71. The Hen nurses its young with wings.
(Kenyang)
Accepting to make the best use of what nature has provided for the security of the young or those put under your care.

72. A house with many children is left open all night.
(Bali, Kenyang)
An assignment left in the hands of children is hardly achieved because no one takes responsibility.

73. The real colour of the hen is seen when the wind blows.
(Lamnso)
Except the wind blows, one wouldn't know that the hen has an anus.
Bakundu, Bakossi, Wimbum variant is: You cannot know a person's secrets except he breaks them to you.

74. If you take shelter in a hut, do not excrete in it.

(Wimbum)

If you receive help from a source, do not block the chances for others in the future.

75. The fortune of a hen is designed by (Kenyang)

Junior or insignificant persons only tumble on luck.

76. We do not hunt using one track. (Wimbum)

Menda-Nkwe variant: If you look at one direction only, your neck will become stiff.

The English variant is: "Do not put all your eggs in one basket."

77. The hand cannot refuse to feed the mouth. (Kenyang, Ejahgam, Bakweri)

It is obligatory to render service to a kinsman.

78. A hasty climber never reaches the top. (Bakweri)

He who eats fast burns his mouth.

(Kenyang)

Hasty climbers have sudden falls

(Menda-Nkwe)

A fast flowing stream does not last.

(Ejahgam)

The English variant is: Patience leads to success or slow and steady wins the race.

79. The value of a knife comes from its handle. (Kenyang)

Ones respect comes from what he does and not what he says or the company he keeps.

M as in Man, Mouse, Marriage, Mother

80. Waker man no di cook canda
(Pidgin)

The traveller puts up with all sorts of hardship the physical strain, little or no food, lack of good facilities, etc.

81. A married man is sure of a nice fufucorn meal.
(Lamnso)

A married man is sure of a square meal. (Traditionally corn, a staple meal in Nso was ground on stone and only a wife could take off time and strain to do that for the husband.)

82. A man's tears do not drop on his chest.
(Kenyang)

Men are expected to be courageous, As a result, they are not expected to carry their problems on their faces.

83. A mother's slap never makes the child ill.
(Mho, Kenyang)

Every loving mother disciplines her child. In the cause of disciplining her child, she cannot harm.

84. What is seen by an old man sitting, the young man standing does not see.
(Mho)

An old man or woman spends many years on earth seeing joy and sorrow, birth and death in brief, many things. The energetic curiosity of the youth tends to move more aggressively over looking certain details that lie around him. In brief, wisdom of grey hair is learnt through experience.

85. The barren mole makes its burrow at the river bank
(Kenyang)
Know yourself no bi kosh. (Krio)
Knowing ones handicaps saves one from a lot of embarrassment.

86. The mouse ploughs the brush while the rat ploughs the house.
(Kenyang, Ejahgam)
Life is made up of adventure and each person embraces it in the way he thinks.

87. Marriage is like washing of hands the one washes the other and vice versa.
(Bakweri)
Marriage is a union of husband and wife, the love that reigns in such a union must be reciprocal.

88. The mouse taught the rat how to steal but the rat has superseded the mouse in stealing.
(Kenyang)
Knowing better than the teacher who taught you.

N as in Nails, Noble.

89. Who will refuse to scratch his own back when he has a hand with nails.
(Kenyang, Bakweri)
Charity begins at home.

90. Nobility differs from wealth.
(Kenyang)
Nobility is inborn while wealth can be acquired or inherited.

O as in Orphan

91. We do not feed an orphan through the nostrils.
(Wimbum)
The advice given to another person's child must be such that can help him/her.

92. Advice to an orphan is given right on the hammock.
(Kenyang)
The Arabic variant is: Advice given in the midst of a crowd is loathsome. Only one who loves you gives you advice. (In giving advice, the intention is to see you do things correctly so that people may credit you. True advice therefore is given in secret. The use of hammock signifies non-secrecy because while on the hammock, the persons are exposed to all the creatures in the river and once advice is not rendered in secret, it becomes mockery or ridicule.)

93. The orphan feeds fat at festivals.
(Kenyang, Esu, Bakweri)
At festivals, there is usually plenty of everything that even paupers get their hare when there are abundance of opportunities.

94. An orphan who survives acquires many parents.
(Kenyang)

When you rise to a good position, you acquire many friends, relatives and well wishers. Human beings like to associate with people of status.

Greek variant: When your wine flask is full, many friends can be made.

95. An orphan is sure of his share when cocoyams are sour.
(Lamnso, Bali)

People without direct parents have only when there is abundance to spare.

Porcupine, Pregnant, Plantain, Pepper, Plum tree, Pond, Palm tree, Prince.

96. Do not hit the porcupine on its nose.
(Kenyang)

A porcupine lives in a burrow. In its attempt to come out of the burrow, it sends out its nose. If you interrupt its outward movement, it will wilfully stay in the burrow. In a dialogue, you are advised not to interrupt the person speaking to you. Rather, you should give him a chance to open up. Always give your opponent the chance to express his ideas fully, otherwise, he/she may hold back some useful information.

97. Because the Porcupine accumulates its grievances, its stomach is bitter.
(Kenyang, Ejahgam)

Anger is self-destructive.

(See bible references. Proverbs 14:17. A patient man has great understanding but a quick-tempered man displays folly.)

If a person conceals a lot of irritating things, it can be harmful to him.

98. A healthy plantain deserves support.
(Kenyang, Nweh)
A hard working person deserves help.

99. When pepper gets finished, you will feed on rat droppings.
(Kenyang, Ejahgam)
(Traditionally dried pepper is stored and preserved in baskets and often, rats get into these baskets. When the pepper is getting finished, there is likelihood that you may pick pepper with rat droppings.)

The proverb means that: If you have had the best from someone at his prime, you should make do with what he provides at old age.

100. If your brother is on the plum tree, you are sure of the ripe ones.
(Kenyang, Ejahgam and most Cameroonian tribes.)
Another variant is: When your brother is on a mango tree, you are sure to have the ripe ones. (Dependence on a godfather.)

101. The Plum tree that bears on one branch.
(Kenyang)
Something that is absurd, in a polygamous home for instance, a husband discovers that only one of his wives is productive or only the children of one woman are intelligent. (An expression of disappointment in nature's imbalance in distribution of productivity or intelligence.)

102. A calm pond is drowning ground.
(Kenyang, Ejahgam, Kijem)
Slow water runs very deep.
Bakweri variant: The dog that looks calm steals.
Wimbum variant: The river that makes little noise takes
away lives.

103. Only tappers know what lies at the nose of the
palm tree.
(Kenyang)
Indian variant: He who bears the burden on his
shoulders knows the weight.
The taste of the pudding is in the eating.
He who wears the shoe knows where it pinches.

104. A prince that coverts the throne ends up losing
it.
(Wimbum)
A man with vaulting ambitions is always the loser at
the end.

105. The cashew dropped just when the porcupine
appeared.
(Kenyang)
Arriving just on time. (Porcupines love cashew nuts,
so if the cashew drops just when the porcupine arrives,
then it has dropped just in time.

106. When labour prolongs, the pregnant woman
does not hide her vagina.
When things become difficult, confidential facts become revealed, no matter how unpleasant.

R as in Rat, Rain, River, Roads, Roofs,
107. The rat's death originates from its burrow.

(Kenyang)
The enemy lies underneath the bed.
Bakweri variant: The thing that beats the drum for Njang is in his own compound.
Menda-Nkwe variant: Plans to kill one often originates from those who live within close quarters.

108. A river that flows alone often meanders.
(Ejahgam, Wimbum, Kenyang, Menda-Nkwe)
You learn from the people with whom you mix with. If you live alone, you often know little. Ngugi Wa Thiong'o argues that in the African view, the community serves the individual. The individual finds the fullest development of his personality when he is working in and for the community as a whole.

109. Rain can bring pigeons, hens and all birds under the same roof.
(Wimbum)
Circumstances can bring all classes of people together.

110. It is the roof **that covers the house.**
(Kenyang, Ejahgam)
The roof covers a lot of things.
Wimbum variant: Problems are manmade. Except you expose your problems and secrets to the public, no one would know.
English variant: washing your dirty linen in public.

111. The road does not inform or warn the traveller.
(Kenyang, Ejahgam)
It is difficult to predict the future.

112. Walk with care, the roads are slippery.

(Kenyang)
(Advice especially to the youths, drawing their attention the fact that looks bright and gay yet pregnant huddles/problems.

113. Do we have to buy a pussycat in a bag?
Pidgin: We di buy pussy for bag?
English variant: Do you buy a tiling without seeing it?

114. Rats that live in a house do not feel the smoke. (Wimbum)
The housemates never dread a problem in a house.

S as in Salt, Servant, Sheep, Shoulder, Snake, Snail, Snuff, Spear.

115. Except you die young, then will you miss the keayaka salt.
(Kenyang, Bakweri)
Except you die young, then will you miss those precious things destined for you. (Keayaka salt is precious salt prepared locally without contamination with chemicals.

116. When the sheep becomes old, it is breast fed by its young.
(Bum)
Child production and nurturing is an investment (There is therefore a hope that when parents grow old they depend on their children for survival.)

117. A spear thrown in anger never hits its target.
(Menda-Nkwe)
Anger is self-destructive. Anything done in anger

hardly goes successfully.

118. When the Iguana is anxious to kill the snail, he will accuse it of having thrown its saliva on him.
(Kenyang)
Give a dog a bad name to hang it.

119. A long snake does not cross a wide road.
(Ejahgam, Bakweri, Kenyang.)
One with extended family ties should avoid conflicts for fear of revenge.

120. The shoulder can never grow above the head.
(Ejahgam, Kenyang, Wimbum, Bakweri, Kom, Oshie, Menda-Nkwe, Esu.)
Things must take their normal and natural order. (Naturally, the shoulder falls below the head. The proverb makes emphasis on respect for hierarchy and experience. African societies work on the assumption that age, rank and experience that comes with it are indispensable to the well being of the community. The longer a man lives and the position that he holds in society, the more experience that he acquires.)

121. One beaten by a snake gets scared when he sees a millipede or earthworm.
(Kenyang, Ejahgam)
The English variant is: Once beaten, twice shy.
Wimbum variant: A burnt child fears wood ash.
Hindustani variant: He who has been scalded with hot milk blows even buttermilk before he drinks it.

122. One person does not grind snuff for a conference.

(Kenyang)
Problems are universal.

123. He who makes friends with the spider cannot be drowned in the river.
If you make friends with people who have the means, you will never suffer or starve. (The proverb teaches togetherness Unity with people who have the means.)

T as in Tiger, trade, Teeth, Toad, Thief, Tree, Toilet, Termites.

124. You do not trade like an ant.
(Bali)
You do not trade on no profit.
Enyang variant: You do not trade like Taku-mu. He sells a dog to buy a dog.

125. The Tiger never changes its marks.
(Bakweri, Duala)
An unpleasant character hardly reforms. Chinese variant: Rotten wood cannot be carved

126. One bad tooth spoils the mouth.
(Bakweri)
The unrighteous penny corrupts the righteous one. One scabbed sheep will mess the whole flock. The rotten apple injures its neighbours
One drop of poison infects a whole turn of wine.
Live with him who prays and you" will pray, live with him who sings and you will sing.
Duala, Kenyang, Kijem, Bakossi variant: One bad cocoyam spoils the fufu.
Bakweri variant: One oily finger soils the rest.

Arab variant: Bad company causes corruption.

The scriptures confirm: "He who walks with the wise grows wise but companion of fools suffer." (Proverbs 13:20)

127. If you keep company with a thief, you will someday steal.

(Kenyang)

Birds of a feather flock together.

128. The adult does not use the same toilet with children.

(Wimbum)

If you want to keep your respect, choose your assignment and partners to match your age.

Kenyang variant: The adult falls from kolanuts trees, a youth can fall from a plum tree.

129. A Tiger's cub does not grow old for its marks to be noticed.

(Wimbum)

A healthy cocoyam is known right from its shoot.

Kenyang variant: A person's character is noticed at its prime.

130. A falling tree is not easily blown down by a storm.

(Kenyang)

What looks feeble/fragile may not necessarily be delicate.

131. The tortoise moves with its house.

(Oshie)

Evidence of self-sufficiency.

132. That which belongs to the toad does not climb a tree.
(Nso)
What is destined for you will fall within your reach someday.

133. The thigh and the hip should not quarrel with each other.
People of the same kin should not quarrel since they are ore body (family)

U as in Urinal.

134. If someone leads you to the urinal, you in turn should lead him to the latrine.
(Kenyang, Ejahgam)
One good turn deserves another.
Kindness pays for kindness.
(Traditionally, toilets are built away from the house and so it becomes frightful paying nature's call alone at certain hours of the day without company. So there is need for a companion.)

W as in Water, Widow, Woman, Walks, Warriors, Womb.

135. A nagging widow would lead you to ridicule or abuse your deceased brother.
(Kenyang, Bakossi, Ejahgam)
(Marriage in these tribes is a family union and a wife is family property. If a husband dies, his next of kin inherits his property including his wife. But love at youth has proved to be long lasting. Quite often, the

widow compares her late husband with the new one and is at times tempted to make derogatory statements against her new husband. Such statements may tempt the new husband to say things against his brother, the deceased.)

English variant: Statements made by an irresponsible person may lead you to make derogatory remarks against your close relative.

136. One who wants a wife must lie on his back.
(Kenyang, Ejahgam)

He who needs a wife should be tolerant and submissive to his in-laws, especially during courtship. (Tolerance and submissiveness is a virtue in marriage.)

137. A woman who sows on fertile soil would rest her basket on her heap.
(Kenyang)

Success breeds success.

138. Any dorty water di loss fire.
(Pidgin, Wimbum)

English variant: A drowning man clutches at a serpent. Any solution is necessary to a desperate person.

139. Walls have ears.
(Wimbum, Bakweri, Kenyang)

Always talk with caution and reservations for fear that any listener could pass the information to the wrong quarters.

Russian variant: A word is like a bird which once flown, you can never catch it.

140. Good wood (for cooking) does not burn till

dawn.

(Bakweri)

A hyperactive life is short lived. (The firewood referred to is the one that is used for cooking unlike the type used for keeping the house warm at night. The kind for cooking is very dry and as such, it burns fast and heats intensively. Consequently, it soon burns out. Hence, it's fraught with hustling and bustling is short lived.)

141. The warrior's purse constantly remains empty.

(Kenyang)

A warrior will never be completely successful. (Normally, one who is troublesome is always quarrelling and fighting and as such will always appear before the courts to pay fines, thereby emptying his purse often.)

Proverbs 29 v 23: Arrogance will bring downfall but if you are humble, you will be respected.

Proverbs 14 v 16: Wise people are careful to stay out of trouble but stupid people are careless and act too quickly.

BIBLIOGRAPHY

David. K. Mphande, *The Use of Malawian proverbs in Moral Instruction and Religion in Malawi* - 1996. (an annual publication produced by the Department of Theology and Religious studies, University of Malawi.)

Ejahgam people, *Our Cultural Heritage "Nkui Ekom Eriaa* Published by the Ejahgam Cultural Association, Buea - 1980.

Fonge Foteh Michael, *Discover Life's Treasures Hidden in African Proverbs where village is the Foundation.* Published by Lebock Publishing, Houston Texas - 1997

Jan Knapperts, *The A-Z of African Proverbs* -Karnak House-1989.

Jick Henry, *Folklore ad National Development: Kom and Bakweri Proverbs.* Limbe design House, 2006.

Kelso J.A. ed., "Proverbs" in Encyclopedia of Religion and Ethics- Vol. 10. New York: T & T

Matute Daniel, *The Socio-cultural Legacies of the Baker is of Cameroon.*

Narma Gleason, *Proverbs from Around The World.* Macmillan 1992.

Ngala Ghiantal, *African Proverbs and Interpretations. (A collection from Wimbum)* Jos: Star-Link Communications - 1997.

Tala Kashim Ibrahim, *An introduction to Cameroon Oral Literature.* Yaounde: SOPECAM- 1984

Zondervan Coroaration, *The Devotional Study Bible.* - 1987.